GREAT GARDENS

of New Zealand

GREAT
GARDENS
of New Zealand

Text and Photography by
Derek Fell

NORTH ISLAND • SOUTH ISLAND • STEWART ISLAND

David Bateman

In memory of my parents:
Albert John Fell and Mary Woodhouse McCafferty

ACKNOWLEDGEMENTS

I wish to thank the many New Zealanders who helped me find memorable gardens to photograph, in particular Robyn Kilty, Christchurch garden designer; Raylene Waddell, Stewart Island gardener; Robin Booth, Kerikeri nurseryman; and garden writers Gordon Collier, Olive Dunn and Alison McRae.

The hardest part of compiling this book was deciding which among the numerous gardens deserving attention to exclude, so there are many garden owners I should thank whose properties I considered but could not include in the final selection because of space limitations.

Many garden owners allowed me to stay as their guest, sometimes for several nights, putting me up in a cottage or bed-and-breakfast facility available to visitors. Availability of homestay accommodation and other details regarding public access are given in an appendix (see page 222) rather than in the main text.

The book involved ten visits to New Zealand, often accompanied by my wife, Carolyn, who greatly assisted me in my research.

Thanks also to Joan Haas, my office manager, for maintaining my photo files and research data and holding the fort while I was away, and to the talented team of designers and editors at David Bateman Ltd for making this book a reality.

PAGE 1: *Tuatara pottery design, Bellevue*
PAGE 2 (AND JACKET): *Maple Glen, Wyndham*
PAGE 4: *Fantail doves, Burnard Garden*
PAGE 7: *Perennial garden with dovecote, Rathmoy*

ABOUT THE AUTHOR

DEREK FELL was born and educated in England. A widely published garden writer and photographer, he now lives in Pennsylvania, USA. Winner of more awards from the Garden Writers' Association than any other person, he first visited New Zealand in 1993, to be married in Auckland, and has returned every year since, documenting New Zealand gardens for publication worldwide. His articles on New Zealand gardens have appeared in *New Zealand Gardener* and numerous international magazines, including *Architectural Digest*, *The Garden* (the magazine of the Royal Horticultural Society), *Hemispheres*, *American Nurseryman* and *Family Circle*.

Fell has judged gardens at a number of flower shows, most recently at the Ellerslie Flower Show, the Pacific Northwest Flower Show, Seattle, and as an international judge for the Floral Villages of France Competition, sponsored by the French Tourism Office.

Married with three children, Fell cultivates an award-winning garden at historic Cedaridge Farm, Pennsylvania, featuring sunny perennial borders, shade gardens, a stream garden and an extensive vegetable garden. The author of more than 90 books and garden calendars, his published works include *Campbell Island — Land of the Blue Sunflowers* (Bateman), *Renoir's Garden* (Frances Lincoln), *The Impressionist Garden* (Frances Lincoln), *Secrets of Monet's Garden* (Barnes & Noble) and *Van Gogh's Gardens* (Simon & Schuster).

Contents

PREFACE

IT IS OBVIOUS why New Zealand gardens like Ayrlies, Trelinnoe Park and Rathmoy, in the North Island, and Larnach Castle, Gethsemane and Maple Glen, in the South, are considered great gardens. The sheer size, quality of plantings and design integrity make these world-class gardens by anyone's standards.

But a book of this scope must consider other criteria, for great gardens need not be big or crammed with flowering plants to have a "wow" factor. Above all I have sought to present *diversity*; diversity not only of style, but also of size and local geography, including hill country, coastal regions and bush. I have also tried to present a good balance of North Island and South Island gardens, and introduce some of the remarkable gardens of Stewart Island, a place with a small population and a reputation for difficult growing conditions.

At the outset I decided the gardens featured in the book should be privately owned, so public gardens like the Eden Garden (Auckland's tropical masterpiece, tended by members of the Eden Garden Society) and Pukeiti (the magnificent rhododendron garden near New Plymouth, maintained by the Pukeiti Rhododendron Trust) have been excluded in spite of their greatness.

New Zealanders plant a lot of bog gardens because of the country's relatively high rainfall, and many gardeners take inspiration from English cottage gardens, so it would be easy to fill a book with these two highly popular and photogenic themes. But to show the extraordinary creativity of New Zealand gardeners I also sought unconventional gardens. For example, Ngamatea is a superb example of a minimalist garden, to be admired for the way the award-winning modernistic house is integrated unobtrusively with the alpine tussock, and native plants (notably grasses) are used to make a smooth transition between the house and the dramatic windswept setting. Appropriately, both house and garden – which display such sensitivity to the indigenous New Zealand landscape – are the work of a great Maori designer.

Westridge and Horrell Gardens are both relatively small – less than half a hectare of steeply sloping terrain – and have a tropical aura, yet respond to their environment in different ways. Westridge is intimate, cosy, largely screened from the outside world, designed for *introspection*, and a wonderful example of a tapestry garden where foliage, rather than flowers, is used to extend colour into the topmost branches so one's entire field of vision is filled with interest. Horrell, on the other hand, exposes itself to the surrounding countryside, encouraging visitors to look out beyond its boundaries. It is a garden of *vistas*, its rich palette of tropical plants interacting with the landscape across the Waipapa River.

The smallest garden, Robyn Kilty's inventive design that hugs three sides of her small cottage in the centre of Christchurch, is included in recognition of its confined central-city setting, the Gaudi influence in its mosaics, and its appealing floral harmonies that take into consideration the colours of the building.

I particularly wanted to show gardens that make dramatic use of native plants, and also elements of New Zealand's pioneering history – for example, the whale pots in the whaling captain's shorefront garden at Butler Point, the gold-mining machinery among the bluebells at Speight Gardens, and the farming implements featured prominently at Rathmoy, one of New Zealand's oldest and largest sheep stations.

The gardens presented here feature both formal and informal designs and are located in both urban and country areas, some of the latter in quite desolate places. Above all, though, they are testimony to New Zealand's rich natural beauty, incredible range of microclimates and their owners' extraordinarily high degree of enthusiasm. These qualities have combined to make gardens that are not only unique and innovative but also among the world's most beautiful.

RIGHT: *Crown ferns, Ulva Island Post Office.*

Introduction
History of New Zealand Gardens

The first European to plant a garden in New Zealand was Captain James Cook, the intrepid British navigator who circumnavigated the globe three times in the 1770s and the first European to step ashore in New Zealand. His first landfall was near Gisborne, on a desolate section of coast dominated by bald cliffs and drifting sand dunes and often ravaged by floods. The prospect of finding food there seemed so poor Cook named that section of coast Poverty Bay, but when he rounded East Cape, to the north, he rejoiced at finding a more fertile area with a plentiful food supply, and named it the Bay of Plenty.

Exploring the two main islands, Cook discovered an even more alluring anchorage in the Marlborough Sounds, close to a sheltered beach rimmed with tree ferns, and a clean freshwater stream cleaving a steep hillside. He landed, set up tents to rest his crew and made repairs to his ship, naming the place Ship Cove.

During a stay of several weeks, Cook supervised the planting of peas, carrots, parsnips, strawberries and wheat, and paid some local Maori to look after them. When he returned to inspect the harvest after an absence of a year, however, he found the local inhabitants had allowed the plots to revert to wilderness, but he was amazed how many of the crops had flourished in spite of neglect.

Maori were naturally suspicious of European food crops, preferring to grow their own staples, such as kumara, taro (a plant with a large edible rootstock), gourds and puha (a soft, leafy thistle they cooked like spinach). Maori had no understanding of the European tradition of individual land ownership, or the concept of a pleasure garden, which the early colonists brought with them. Their perspective was more communal. The iwi was their social community, sustaining them emotionally and physically and maintaining tribal territorial boundaries. The natural environment, both land and sea, were sacred to them as a source of food, and they were fiercely protective of their territory. They saw no reason to control it for aesthetic pleasure for it was already beautiful beyond anything they could visualise.

Today, the Marlborough Sounds remain largely unpopulated. Water taxis from Picton carry visitors to see the monument at Ship Cove commemorating Cook's visit. Bush trails, such as the 71-kilometre Queen Charlotte Walkway, connect a few scattered residents, most of them with food and flower gardens bountiful beyond anything Cook could have dreamed possible, for the area not only produces harvests of cool-season crops such as cabbage and broad beans, but also supports orchards of frost-tender lemon and grapefruit trees.

When Marianne North, a Victorian botanical illustrator, visited New Zealand in 1881, a hundred years after Cook's first visit, she arrived at Bluff by steamship from Australia. She expressed pleasure not only at the prevalence of wild flax along the side of the road into Invercargill, but also at the comfortable accommodation at Gerrard's Hotel, still located near the railway station. She visited Queenstown, where she painted cabbage trees and spear grass against the backdrop of the snow-capped Remarkables mountain range and the glittering aquamarine waters of Lake Wakatipu. But Dunedin dampened her spirits. The hotel in residential Leith was small and depressing. It poured with rain and blew a gale during her entire stay. She was stricken with rheumatism and never set foot on the beautiful Otago Peninsula. "I was half dead and starved when I reached Christchurch," she complained in her diary. She was "sick of everything belonging to that cold, heartless stony island."

When North boarded a steamer for Wellington, she wrote, "I was ill and miserable." In Wellington she stayed with the British governor and his wife, who sympathised with her

ABOVE: *Olive Dunn's garden, Invercargill.*
RIGHT: *Glenfalloch Garden, Dunedin, emulates a Scottish bog garden.*

discomfort, and she found the strength to journey by rail three hours up the Kapiti Coast, where she "crawled" into a garden and obtained "good studies of the nikau palm, the most southern of all palms".

In Auckland North was relieved to board the steamship *Zealandia* for San Francisco and an exploration of the North American Pacific coast.

Seaman Frank Bullen received a quite different impression of New Zealand during the same period when his ship, the American whaler *Splendid*, put in at Kororareka (now Russell), in Northland. New Zealand's first flower gardens were planted there by Scottish missionaries. Dubbed "the hell hole of the South Pacific" at the height of the whaling industry, Kororareka had an unsavoury population of ex-convicts from Britain's penal colonies and deserters from American whaling ships, who preyed on seamen and catered to visiting whalers with grog shops and brothels. Yet beyond the town's lawless beachfront were streets of neat gingerbread cottages with colourful gardens so beautiful they prompted Bullen to make note of them in his famous whaling saga, *Cruise of the Cachalot*. By the time he arrived in Kororareka, its glory days

as a whaling port were on the wane, and Bullen described it as "a maritime sleepy hollow". However, it still had its shady characters who could rob a drunken seaman, so when his crew were granted shore leave he organised a picnic to keep them away from the local low life and preserve their pay. As he reported: "I remember vividly how, just after we got clear of town, we were turning down a lane between hedgerows wonderfully like one of our country roads in England, when

BELOW LEFT: *Colonial-style flower beds at the historic Waitangi Treaty House, Northland, surround a mature native cabbage tree. English cottage garden annuals — such as calendulas, cineraria daisies and snapdragons — are enclosed by a low, evergreen boxwood hedge.*

BELOW RIGHT: *The historic Stone Store at Kerikeri, Northland, with a productive colonial-style vegetable garden featuring English runner beans on poles in the foreground.*

RIGHT: *Historic Fyffe Cottage, Kaikoura, South Island, features a small cottage garden, with whale vertebra used as a decorative accent and symbol of New Zealand's whaling heritage.*

something gripped my heart and sent a lump in my throat. Tears sprang unbidden to my eyes, and I trembled from head to foot with emotion."

What had caught his eye was a hedge laden with English hawthorn blossom, its sweet scent reminding him of London streets, where it grew even among the dockyard slums. "But to me who had not seen a bit of it for years the flood of feeling undimmed by that odorous breath was overwhelming. I could hardly tear myself away from that lovely spot, and when at last I did, I found myself continually turning to try and catch another whiff of one of the most beautiful scents in the world."

The early European settlers found most New Zealand native plants, such as cabbage trees, nikau palms and tree ferns, alien in appearance, even threatening. They considered them nuisance plants, part of the bush they had to chop down and clear to gain a foothold. They filled their gardens with comforting British cottage plants grown easily from seed, such as poppies and sweet peas. They especially cherished roses and geraniums brought from the "old country" as rooted cuttings.

As Bullen walked towards a picnic bench with his shipmates, the sight of more flowers continued to pull at his heartstrings. "Presently we came to a cottage flooded from ground to roof with blossoms of scarlet geranium. There must have been thousands of them, all borne by one huge stem which was rooted by the door of the house," he marvelled.

He also described, in front of the geranium, a fuchsia, about four metres high, its widespread branches loaded with handsome, pendant, orange-red blooms, while the ground beneath was carpeted with petals shaken from the stems by the wind. Bullen returned to the ship with flowers, oysters gathered from the shore and most of his money still in his pocket. He described himself as "full of happy memories of one of the most delightful days of our whole lives".

Today, Russell's quaint Victorian cottage gardens are still bounded by hawthorn hedges. The Mediterranean climate allows geraniums and fuchsias to over-winter with ease, and within the 300-kilometre bight of the Bay of Islands can be found some fine coastal gardens. Two of historical significance are at Kemp House, in Kerikeri – the earliest surviving homestead in New Zealand, dating back to 1821 – and the Treaty House, in Waitangi. Both are beautiful colonial-style gardens, with flower-beds and vegetable plots.

RIGHT: *Rock garden at the Dunedin Botanical Garden in spring, with drifts of pink rock jasmine and magenta creeping phlox in the foreground and deep pink sea pinks in the background.*

In the South Island, a more frugal historic residence is Fyffe House, in Kaikoura, the cottage of a shore whaler, George Fyffe, who arrived from Scotland in 1854. Scattered about the flower gardens are relics from New Zealand's early pioneering days, including bleached whalebones. Even the foundation piles of Fyffe House are composed of whale vertebrae. Similarly, in the gold-mining regions of central Otago and Westland, relics of pioneer times are used as functional garden ornaments – metal wagon wheels to form the hand rails of a bridge leading to a hill-country homestead, for instance, and an assortment of farming and gold-mining implements to make a fence around a former gold prospector's cottage at Ross, where an open-pit gold mine still operates.

The first of New Zealand's many botanical gardens was established in Dunedin in 1863 on what is now the campus of the University of Otago. It was transferred to its present hilly 32-hectare site in Leith in 1886 after the Leith Stream flooded. The new site allowed for a greater number of plants to be grown in two distinct areas, known as the upper and lower gardens. The upper garden is largely wooded and contains such a vast collection of rhododendrons the city holds an annual rhododendron festival at the end of October.

Creating a beautiful transition between the upper and lower gardens, on a sunny slope above Lindsay Creek, is the Rock

Garden. Covering 2000 square metres, this took seven years to build. Claimed to be the largest temperate rock garden in the world, it uses basalt from Mount Cargill for its rock "outcrops". A gravel path zigzags up through the Rock Garden to a rhododendron dell and the topmost part of the ridge, which is devoted mostly to native plants – tall spires of lancewood, tussock grasses, cabbage trees, and rata that cover themselves with crimson bristle-brush flowers at Christmas time.

New Zealand's largest conservatory complex, known as the Winter Garden, is in Auckland Domain. Of two domed glass buildings either side of a courtyard, one features an impressive display of temperate flowering plants, the other tropicals. Adjacent to the Winter Garden is a new facility, the Fernz Fernery, a gully featuring New Zealand's largest collection of native ferns.

Since many early immigrants came from Great Britain, early New Zealand gardens were planted along the lines expounded by Victorian garden writers such as Gertrude Jekyll and William Robinson. Even today, New Zealand gardeners flock to lectures by visiting British gardening dignitaries such as Christopher Lloyd, Helen Dillon and Beth Chatto, who carry on the colour themes and the traditions of mixed perennial borders and woodland and water gardens espoused by Jekyll. But probably the most important inspiration of these overseas experts has been the adoption of New Zealand native plants. Once chastised for not making greater use of native species, New Zealanders have now developed such a strong appreciation of them that numerous specialist native-plant nurseries cater for demand, and even commercial institutions have embraced the idea of a native-plants garden. One of the most unusual can be seen at the Polynesian Spa, Rotorua, surrounding a natural hot pool, a rubber membrane beneath the soil protecting the roots of hebes, toetoe, lancewood and other natives from the region's volcanic gases.

Perhaps the best place to evaluate the potential of New Zealand natives is the Otari Native Plants Garden, on Wilton Road, Wellington. Situated on the slopes of a gully, it features the country's largest collection of native plants, many displayed in a series of "idea gardens" that demonstrate different ways of using them.

ABOVE LEFT: *Thermal pool planted exclusively with native plants at the Polynesian Spa, Rotorua.*
RIGHT: *Temperate house at Auckland's Winter Garden, where temperate plants such as delphiniums and foxgloves are partnered with sub-tropicals like spider plants, howea palms and spires of giant lobelia.*

Native and introduced plants can be intermingled to telling effect. This is particularly true in Auckland and Northland, where winters are virtually frost-free and gardeners can take inspiration from the bold tropical creations of Brazilian landscape architect the late Roberto Burle Marx. For clients around Rio de Janeiro, Marx used great sweeps of drought-tolerant tropical plants, such as giant bromeliads, monstera philodendron vines and silvery succulents, to colour their gardens.

Analytically, New Zealand gardens fall into four broad categories: hill-country, coastal, bush and urban. Hill-country gardens generally occur around homesteads on sheep stations,

particularly in Canterbury and Hawke's Bay. They often differ from farm gardens in other countries by exhibiting a high degree of design sophistication as a result of the landowner being fairly affluent and employing a professional landscape designer.

A significant influence in the design of hill-country gardens is Christchurch landscape architect Alfred Buxton (1872–1950), active in the early 1900s. Born in Staffordshire, England, Buxton emigrated to New Zealand and started a nursery. Having developed a sound knowledge of plants before becoming a landscape designer, he gave many homesteads a flavour of English pastoral elegance to evoke memories of the

"old country". The garden he designed at Garvan Homestead, South Otago, features a number of his favourite elements: a long driveway bordered by trees that screen the property so the homestead is revealed only at the last moment, exotic trees chosen for their dramatic flowering effects, such as laburnums, and weeping trees, particularly Camperdown elm. The property also features a shrubbery, a rock garden, a hazelnut walk (shades of Gertrude Jekyll) and a wildlife pond.

Even with his English upbringing Buxton adapted his designs to New Zealand's unique landscape and pre-dominantly Mediterranean climate, consciously integrating indigenous and introduced plants.

Early settlers frequently had to tame a much more rugged landscape than England's rolling hills, and although New Zealand farms stocked a lot of sheep, these were not seen as a picturesque element as on many English estates, but purely as a means of economic survival. Hence sheep were largely excluded from vistas. Shelter-belts of fast-growing evergreen trees, such as macrocarpa and radiata pine (or Monterey cypress and Monterey pine respectively), were planted round homesteads to cushion them from the wind. These also effectively shut out the wild landscape and sheep pasture, creating oases of Englishness.

Today, the appreciation of native plants is so strong that rather than screening out the wilderness, New Zealanders value it, situating gardens to take advantage of scenic elements beyond their boundaries. A bush walk today is a status symbol.

New Zealand coastal gardens are abundant as a result of so many residential properties being built along the coastline, one of the longest of any island nation, and the ninth longest of any country in the world. Surprisingly, considering it has a permanent population of less than 400 residents, the largest concentration of coastal gardens is on Stewart Island, with New Zealand's southernmost garden located on offshore Ulva Island.

New Zealand coastal gardens differ from those in other countries largely because a vast number of flowering plants can thrive close to the surf as a result of coastal mists and frequent rainfall drenching the sandy soil, and thanks to the extraordinary salt tolerance of macrocarpa and radiata pine. Without the shelter they provide many colourful New Zealand coastal gardens could not exist.

Several influential New Zealand garden writers have promoted distinctive designs. Gordon Collier, founder of the spectacular bush garden at Titoki Point, near Taihape, created a garden in a gully that has received international acclaim for its sensitive integration of native and introduced plants. Although Collier recently retired and sold the property to his

niece, the garden has reopened and remains inspirational as one of New Zealand's first bush gardens, impressing with its strong textural contrasts provided by the foliage of native plants such as cabbage trees and tree ferns.

A similar appreciation of textural and sculptural contrasts using foliage is evident in the garden designs of New Zealand landscape architect Anthony Paul, based in London. He introduced some fresh elements into English garden design in the 1980s and 1990s by emphasising foliage contrasts with formal water features, bold paving and minimal use of colour.

Recently, even the Royal Horticultural Society has endorsed use of the word *Kiwiana* to describe a space infused with New Zealand plants and structural accents. The idea sprang from New Zealander James Fraser's design for artist Biddy Bunzl's city garden in Breakspears Road, south-east London.

LEFT: *Naturalistic wildlife pond at Otari Native Plants Garden, Wellington, features an alpine tussock,* Chionochloa flavicans, *conspicuously on the cliff face.*
BELOW: *New Zealand-bred Oriental lily 'Casablanca' is highly fragrant and a popular cut flower.*

Favouring New Zealand natives such as silvery sword-shaped astelias interspaced with tufted hair sedge and rainbow grass, Fraser introduced new visual sensations to staid British tastes, mostly using plant textures and forms rarely seen in Britain. Trees are pruned bare of their lower branches to emphasize truncated forms, like New Zealand's lancewood and black tree ferns and the snaking trunks of cabbage trees. Tussock grasses beneath create an airy, windblown, heathlike aspect. This fleecelike under-storey is threaded with meandering paths of gravel and crushed shells leading to raised walkways of irregular planks, suggestive of the boardwalks sometimes constructed to traverse New Zealand bogs. Weatherworn planks, also of irregular lengths – as though salvaged from the beach – are set on end to create rustic boundary fences.

Olive Dunn's cottage garden, in Invercargill, was an inspiration to thousands of gardeners – not only those who visited, but the many others who read her lively articles in the *New Zealand Gardener* before she retired in 1996. Although

Olive still maintains a garden, it is now closed to visitors. Her several books on gardening and floral crafts were bestsellers, and her *Cottage Gardening in New Zealand* calendar for many years presented scenes from her garden through four seasons. As a result of her prolific writing she became to New Zealand what Penelope Hobhouse is to Britain, possessing acute colour sensitivity and taking much inspiration from Gertrude Jekyll and the French Impressionist painters.

An aspect of New Zealand's garden heritage often overlooked is the breeding and introduction of new plants that have become popular both in New Zealand and abroad. The late John Eaton developed the 'Rainbow' variety of silver beet, and worked on a special selection that enabled Johnny's Seeds, in the USA, to win an All-America Award for 'Bright Lights', which features 11 distinct colours, including white, scarlet, orange, yellow, lemon, apricot and pink, as well as striped varieties.

Rosarian Sam McGredy, who began breeding in Ireland, recognised the benefits of New Zealand's climate for superior rose-growing and moved his breeding activities to Auckland. 'Sexy Rexy', a vigorous, disease-resistant, award-winning shrub rose, is one of McGredy's more famous New Zealand introductions, now sold worldwide.

The highly fragrant 'Casablanca' oriental lily – now the world's most popular florist flower – was developed from a breeding programme run by Dr John Stuart Yeates (1900–1986) at Massey University, while the vigorous, late-flowering 'Hawera' miniature daffodil was discovered by a Taranaki doctor. Hybridising of New Zealand flax has produced numerous colourful varieties, now making a big impact on gardens in California and Great Britain, especially those introduced by Margaret Jones at her nursery near Rotorua. Work by New Zealanders on dahlias, camellias, rhododendrons, delphiniums and sweet peas has also received international acclaim. Of particular note is the part played by Ilam Homestead, Christchurch, in the breeding of azaleas and rhododendrons that have become world famous.

Ilam Homestead is now a clubhouse for staff at the University of Canterbury, and the grounds are open to the public. Each spring the property becomes a flowering paradise as drought-tolerant hybrid azaleas developed by an early owner, Edgar Stead, burst into bloom. When Stead discovered Christchurch was a perfect climate for growing azaleas he began crossing Britain's 'Knap Hill' hybrids with several North American species. Such well-known varieties as 'Persian Melon', 'Ilam Alarm', 'Ilam Cerise', 'Ilam Cream' and 'Irene Stead' feature among streamside and woodland plantings, many of them grown into tall trees.

New Zealand is famous for its kiwifruit and apple orchards

and its beautiful vineyards. Less well known is its production of cut flowers for export, with orchids top of the list. Even tropical water lilies are now an export item, with Wright's Water Gardens, at Pukekohe, growing them in outdoor ponds for export to Europe and America as a cut flower. Timaru has become a centre for the production of calla, or arum, lilies for cutting, and several peony farms in the South Island produce cut peonies for export. Because of New Zealand's antipodean seasons, the production of cut flowers seems boundless.

Indeed, the most exciting part of New Zealand's garden history is still in the making. With a recent infusion of government funding into the arts and heritage areas, and a ban on logging most native forest, New Zealand is likely to become even better known as a great gardening nation – perhaps even the greatest.

LEFT: *Ilam Homestead Garden, Christchurch, features a series of streams crossed by several Monet-style bridges, and a spectacular collection of rhododendrons among native plants, including wheki tree ferns, cabbage trees (*Cordyline australis*) and flax.*
ABOVE: *Orange gerbera daisies contrast harmoniously with indigo blue walls surrounding a courtyard at an Ellerslie Flower Show garden exhibit.*

North Island GARDENS

NORTH ISLAND GARDENS tend to fall into two categories: subtropical and temperate. Auckland and Northland generally enjoy balmy, frost-free winters and hot, humid summers, allowing gardeners to grow exotic plants outdoors, including banana trees, cymbidium orchids and bromeliads.

South of Auckland the climate is more temperate, with sharper winters and many areas being touched by frost. As a consequence, gardens feature hardier plants such as rhododendrons, roses, witch hazels, bog primulas and saucer magnolias.

The most prolific native North Island flowering plant species is the New Zealand "Christmas tree", the pohutukawa (*Metrosideros excelsa*). Common along the coast, this displays masses of scarlet bristly flowers at Christmas time. However, the single most prolific flowering plant throughout the North Island is the blue lily of the Nile, *Agapanthus africanus*, an African immigrant that has colonised vast stretches of sandy and gravelly soil, especially along the coast.

LEFT: *Blue and white African agapanthus drift down a sand dune to the water's edge at Hokianga Harbour, Northland.*

Butler Point

Mangonui – Home of the Shark

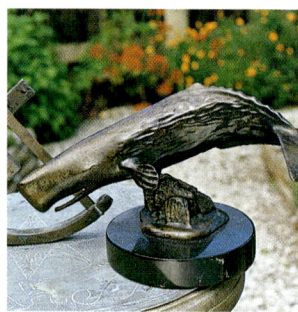

In 1828, when he was just 14 years old, William Butler, of Dorset, rebelled against his clergyman father's wishes to enter the ministry and ran away to sea. By age 24 he was captain of the Sydney whaling brig *Nimrod*, which put in at Mangonui Harbour, north of the Bay of Islands. Butler noted how the captains of American whalers preferred Mangonui (Maori for "home of the shark") to the nearby whaling port of Kororareka (now Russell) because it had no grog shops or brothels, so their crews were less likely to desert. As many as 40 whalers at a time used the safe, sheltered, frost-free harbour, where they traded with friendly Maori for kumara, shellfish and pork.

RIGHT: *View from the shorefront garden at Butler Point, Northland, where whaling captain William Butler established a self-sufficient homestead.*
ABOVE: *Bronze sculpture of a sperm whale is part of a collection of whaling artefacts at the Butler Point whaling museum.*

LEFT: *Garden gate leading from the old Butler homestead to the shorefront, with a ponga fence to provide shelter from coastal winds and salt spray.*

ABOVE LEFT: *Pendant, orange, bell-shaped bloom of Indian mallow grows on a frost-tender shrub.* (RIGHT): *Scarlet blooms of* Erythrina caffra *grow on leafless trees in early spring.*

TOP RIGHT: *Arbour of* Bougainvillea *shades a path of crushed oyster shells beside the old Butler homestead.*

BOTTOM RIGHT: *Tubular orange blooms of* Aloe mitriformis *and pink flower stem of* Beschorneria yuccoides *edge an exposed shorefront path leading to more sheltered gardens.*

Butler bought land on a forested peninsula facing Mangonui's waterfront and established a comfortable self-sufficient homestead to start a family, farm the land and provision the visiting whalers. He not only supplied spars and masts, he also raised chickens, pigs and cattle, grew acres of fresh vegetables, and traded flax and kauri gum. He learned to speak Maori, earned the respect of local chiefs and acted as a magistrate in settling disputes among the colonists. He also served the community as a doctor, pilot, chemist, banker and lay reader, even representing his district as a Member of Parliament.

Today, the Mangonui waterfront retains many features of the whaling era, while the house, store and outbuildings Butler built along a crescent of beach in the lee of the peninsula have been faithfully restored by present owners Lindo and Laetitia Ferguson. Now known as Butler Point, the 24-hectare estate has been converted into a private whaling museum and shorefront garden, which can be visited by appointment.

Only a narrow channel separates Butler Point from Mangonui, but to drive to the estate means making an eight-kilometre circuit of the harbour, the meandering coast road providing exhilarating views at every turn, the tops of the hills often swirling in mist or spotlighted by shafts of golden sunlight.

The last stretch of gravel road dips to the beach of the small coastal community of Hihi, passes through thickets of

mangrove, then steeply ascends a hill into regenerating native bush, once kauri forest. After the immense kauri trees were cut down for timber, the area grew thick with manuka and tree ferns, the branches and fronds of which arch over the narrow road to form a verdant tunnel. As the road crests the promontory it skirts a sunny amphitheatre of 500 macadamia trees, their nuts a source of income for the Fergusons and food for flocks of game birds, including pheasant.

The road then enters a cathedral-like grove of gigantic pohutukawa trees, some estimated to be 700 years old. Aerial roots coil like snakes around the fissured trunks, the immense, spreading, lichen-covered branches extending up and over a fenced cemetery, where Captain Butler lies buried. He was mortally injured in 1875 when he slipped on a jetty and was crushed between a launch and the jetty pilings.

The road sweeps round the cemetery in a wide arc and down to a beach and the old Butler homestead, where a black ponga fence shelters the cottage garden from coastal winds. A pair of metal cauldrons, once used to render down whale blubber, gape from a clump of angelica, and a whaleboat under a wooden canopy flanks the old storehouse-turned-museum. Even a wall of rounded stones along the foreshore is made from the ballast of ships that traded in whale oil. A picket fence garlanded with red fuchsias and ivy-leaf geraniums helps shelter a lawn bordered with other salt-tolerant plants, including grey-leaf cardoons. Set back against a fern-clad slope is a magnificent grandiflora magnolia dating back to 1840. Paths of crushed oyster shell pass beneath rose-covered arbours that provide access to a series of shorefront gardens, terminating at a one-room guest cottage shaded by tall mamaku tree ferns, the under-storey spangled with cineraria daisies.

A particularly appropriate decorative structure in one of the beachfront gardens is a thatched shelter – a low whare – containing an assortment of tools and plant pots.

FAR LEFT: *Thatched Maori-style shelter serves as a storage shed in the shorefront garden, with a colony of* Agave attenuata *in the foreground.*

LEFT: *Tangled branches of a 700-year-old pohutukawa tree (*Metrosideros excelsa*) radiate in all directions from a fallen trunk that has rooted to keep the giant alive.*

ABOVE: *An immense avenue of pohutukawa trees creates a high, wide tunnel like the nave of a cathedral.*

BELOW: *Burial ground among pohutukawa trees, where Captain Butler was interred after his accidental death.*

Inland, the garden slopes up steeply towards a hill still recognisably a pa. The top of the terraced hill fort once accommodated 200 people behind stockade fences, and today provides a panoramic view of the entire peninsula.

"When we purchased the property in 1970, the gardens were overgrown and the original homestead in need of major repair, almost hidden by native bush," Lindo remembers. "Rather than live in the Butler home we decided to build a separate residence on the ridge above, in harmony with the Victorian architecture of the old homestead. It has been extremely satisfying to restore a part of New Zealand's history that could easily have been lost, and to maintain a link with the country's whaling heritage."

The rescue of the garden has been an ongoing commitment. Working systematically outwards from the homestead, the Fergusons chopped back the encroaching bush to bring light and air to old established ornamental trees that were nearing suffocation. The grandiflora magnolia was in such a sad state a professional dendrologist had to conduct major surgery and remedial care so that it could revive and flower again. Another plant treasure saved from neglect is a rare native shrub, *Elingamita johnsonii*. Planted by a former owner, this displays generous clusters of red berries and lustrous green leaves. Pathways long vanished were also restored, and an old brick well in the north garden was excavated.

The focus on whaling, with the whaleboat and cauldrons used as decorative elements, ensures the estate retains much of its old-time aura. Even the room interiors are authentic to the period during which Captain Butler lived in comfort and prosperity surrounded by his 14-member family. Passing through the gates of the Butler Point estate today is like stepping back 150 years.

FAR LEFT: *Pair of metal cauldrons, used for rendering blubber into oil, reminders of Butler Point's whaling heritage and an appropriate decorative accent at the start of the shorefront garden.*
TOP LEFT: *Abyssinian banana,* Ensete ventricosa, *adds an exotic tropical accent to Butler Point's shorefront garden.*
MIDDLE LEFT: *A thatched shelter provides a place to picnic at Butler Point.*
BOTTOM LEFT: *Silverbeet is ready for picking in the colonial-style herb and vegetable garden, situated close to the kitchen at the old Butler homestead.*

Horrell Garden

Soil Science Conquers a Challenging Site in Kerikeri

The rugged coastline and gentle hills of Kerikeri – a Maori word meaning "stony place" – attracted early European settlers for their warm, subtropical climate and proximity to the Bay of Islands, which Captain Cook declared one of the finest anchorages he had ever encountered. The area also supported the largest Maori population in New Zealand. Kumara were grown in plots that sometimes covered several acres, although today Kerikeri is more famous for the great quantities of kiwifruit, citrus and tamarillos it produces.

ABOVE: *Chinese hibiscus blossom.*
RIGHT: *View from the top terrace looking down to the Waipapa River, with a Norfolk Island pine and Australian bottlebrush shrub framed by the arching banana-like leaves of a giant bird of paradise,* Strelitzia nicolai. *Insets show red ginger (top), bicolored amaryllis (center) and Poor Knights lily (*Xeronema callistemon*).*

Kerikeri also has a reconstructed Maori village and a native-plants garden – the Discoverers' Garden – featuring a collection of Northland's most important indigenous plants, including a grove of nikau palms (the leaves of which are used for thatch), rimu (an evergreen timber tree that produces durable shingles and weatherboard) and the kaka beak bush, which Maori women liked for its scarlet blossoms, used as a hair decoration, and which they planted around their dwellings.

Little more than a kilometre from the Discoverers' Garden, which gets its name from the succession of famous botanists the region attracted, starting with Joseph Banks, who accompanied Captain Cook on his first voyage, are the home and garden of John and Judy Horrell. The garden displays a wealth of tropical plants on a cliff so steep it seems impossible anything could gain a foothold there. But the Horrells decided the property was the ideal place to live after attending a party there and discovering it was for sale.

They describe themselves as enthusiastic novice gardeners, Judy claiming responsibility for planting immediately around the house, while John's domain is the labyrinth of steep paths and terraces that zigzag down the slopes to the riverbank. Judy also orchestrates the colour harmonies, especially combinations of pink and blue, and blue and yellow. "Blue is such a good colour for our garden," she explains, "because it echoes the sky and the surrounding water, connecting the cultivated parts of the garden with the surrounding natural landscape."

John is involved in soil management, selling a range of products to balance agricultural soils, and describes his garden as an outdoor laboratory. "It doesn't matter how rich the soil is or how abundant the rainfall, the ultimate health and vigour of plants is the amount of energy they receive from the sun," he says.

The garden's exposure at the end of a promontory and its 12-metre elevation ensure good all-around light, so all that's needed from John is an appropriate fertiliser boost, which he provides with a mixture of molasses and seaweed concentrate, spraying it onto the plants as a foliage feed. John considers molasses the key to his amazing results because it feeds beneficial soil micro-organisms that manufacture a feast of plant nutrients over extended periods.

To gain access to the steep cliff, John has built terraces to carry paths, connected by steps and boardwalks. Stones for the construction of retaining walls were carted to the site from a farmer's lava field. Except for a 400-year-old puriri tree (*Vitex lucens*), the Horrells have planted virtually everything – even New Zealand natives such as nikau palms. For the first three years they went on a buying spree, patronising local tropical-

plants nurseryman Robin Booth, but now they do a lot of dividing of established colonies to expand the garden. As John explains: "For a good tropical effect it's essential to have exotic leaves and colourful plants at eye level, so we have provided supports for ornamental vines in the form of columns and trellises. Some of our favourites are the deep-blue Brazilian sandpaper vine [*Petrea volubilis*] and pale-blue *Thunbergia grandiflora*, from India. Both bloom for several months."

John also enjoys the jungle-like atmosphere that several leafy vines add to a courtyard, including the Swiss cheese vine (*Monstera deliciosa*) and Brazilian tree philodendron (*Philodendron selloum*).

The Horrells' house sits snugly below a cliff overhang, and is approached down a steep driveway through a gatehouse with a guest apartment above it. Fiery-red, giant-flowered amaryllis line the car park in spring. A curving pergola leads from the entrance to the front door, skirting a sheltered courtyard featuring a collection of bromeliads, especially *vriesias*, with zebra-striped leaves, and *neoregelias*, with pink and blood-red arching leaves.

On the sunniest side of the pergola, cliff-edge beds billow with the frothy pink blooms of angel-wing begonias, old garden roses, heat-resistant vireya rhododendrons, stag-horn ferns and a mature bird-of-paradise palm, *Strelitzia nicolai*.

Although the Horrells have installed irrigation they haven't had to use it in three years. John believes his system of mulching beds heavily with radiata-pine chips not only helps to conserve soil moisture, but adds to the soil's humus content as the mulch breaks down. Also, in areas where the soil tends to dry out quickly, he has planted drought-tolerant succulents such as *Aeonium arboreum* 'Zwartkop', with dark maroon – almost black – rosettes.

The Horrells' garden has been only ten years in the making, yet seems much older because of rapid growth due to abundant sunlight and soil fertility. "It's an ideal place for living," John concludes. "When it rains it pours, and the year-round temperature is stable, with no frost. We have a dock at the base of the cliff and a riverboat we call *The African Queen*, and it's such a thrill to be able to walk down to our dock, start up the engine and chug off up or down the estuary for a day's fishing and a picnic at some deserted beach. The whole of the Bay of Islands is accessible to us."

The only aspect of the garden John would change would be to have a vegetable garden where Judy currently has a cottage garden, but since this is directly in front of the living-room window he gives in to Judy's preference. "Teamwork counts for a lot," he admits.

ABOVE: *Fruiting stems of a native nikau palm form a skirt above a colony of drought-tolerant hens-and-chicks (*Echeveria elegans*), with views of Kerikeri Inlet in the background.*
LEFT: *Collection of exotic bromeliads, including* Vriesia hieroglyphica zebrina, *are part of a tropical courtyard planting.*

Bellevue

Colour Echoes in a Coastal Garden

There is probably no dream more common among gardeners born in a temperate climate than to live above a frost-free, powder-soft beach, with views of a glittering blue sea and rocky headlands. Born in Lancashire, in north-west England, where cold winds, freezing rain, thick cloud and deep winter snow can thwart the best attempts at gardening, Vivien Papich has fulfilled her dream of living in a maritime paradise only to discover that the difficulties of a Lancashire garden have been replaced by savage coastal storms, stinging salt spray and summer drought. But the consolation is that after a storm has passed, plants are quick to recover, and any devastation is an opportunity to try something completely different.

ABOVE: *Clump of hens-and-chicks colonize a planter decorated with a tuatara, New Zealand's unique reptile species.*
RIGHT: *View over the golden garden at Bellevue, looking out along the Pacific coastline towards Whangarei Heads, Northland.*

LEFT: *Cymbidium orchids sheltered from coastal winds by variegated cabbage trees.*

INSET: *Sprays of cymbidium orchids arch over a rustic garden bench along the entrance drive.*

TOP: *View of the golden garden with pavilion in the background.*

ABOVE: *Mass planting of hens-and-chicks (*Echeveria secunda*) in company with spiny African aloes, purple-leaf cabbage trees, silvery astelia and black mamaku tree ferns.*

Located on the east coast of Northland, above Lang's Beach, with a clear view of Whangarei Heads, Bellevue house and garden are approached along a steep driveway arched over by the sinuous branches of manuka and pohutukawa. The dark leafy tunnel is a haven for cymbidium orchids, which, in early spring, raise their exotic flower stems above colonies of ferns and bromeliads. But this shady entrance is deceptive, for it is in dramatic contrast to the rest of the property – a spacious, sun-drenched garden laid out on several levels above and below the house.

The property was purchased in 1986, and the garden developed in stages by Vivien, with help from her mother, Ivy, and husband, Daniel. Vivien took responsibility for the overall design and plantings, Ivy helped with pruning and weeding, and Daniel hauled to the site truckloads of topsoil and compost to improve the impoverished indigenous sandy soil. However, a garden that began with overtones of an English cottage garden, including masses of roses and common English seaside fare such as nasturtiums, petunias and crane's-bills, has given way over the years to mass plantings of tropicals and drought-tolerant plants such as native grasses, African wildflowers like agapanthus, and Mexican succulents, including aloes and sedums. As a consequence, the garden has a dry-climate ambience, with carefully orchestrated colour harmonies to intensify its brilliance.

Almost dazzling in its brightness is Vivien's golden garden, sheltered between the north side of the house and a summerhouse. Composed of plants with yellow, gold and orange foliage, it includes gold-lace evergreen cypresses, golden sedge grasses and a rare orange form of North American pitcher plant, *Sarracenia rubra,* which colonises the edges of a pool where even goldfish add to the gold overtones. The gold theme is carried round the front of the house with plantings of gold-leaf jade plants and fruiting citrus in pots. Most ingenious is the way Vivien has draped fishermen's nets of golden thread over a large, prostrate driftwood tree trunk and an adjacent mass planting of sand-dune coprosma (*Coprosma acerosa*), an indestructible drought-tolerant native shrub with a low-growing tight knit of interlocking branches that perfectly echoes the fine mesh of the netting.

Another sophisticated touch is the combination of a blue urn and blue sedum with amber tussock grasses and maroon cabbage trees, the smooth lines of the urn creating a beautiful contrast with the spikiness of the cabbage tree and grass leaves.

A walk through the garden is a visual adventure, a labyrinth of paths leading off from the house uphill and downhill, with places to rest along the way. In a clearing among plantings of agaves and aloes are a slab table and benches made by Daniel

ABOVE: *Naturalistic pool is surrounded with golden-hued plants as part of a large golden garden.*

LEFT: *A North American pitcher plant (*Sarracenia rubra*), colonises a dish planter beside the pond.*

OPPOSITE, TOP LEFT: *Purple-leafed cabbage trees, amber tussock grasses and silvery-blue succulents complement a blue urn on a dry slope.*

OPPOSITE, TOP RIGHT: *Blue bench echoes the blue of succulent blue chalk sticks (*Senecio serpens*) with giant* Aeonium arboreum *'Zwartkop' and purple-leaf cabbage trees providing bold leaf contrasts.*

OPPOSITE, CENTRE: *African aloe provides a strong textural contrast with cushion-shaped clumps of succulents, including hens-and-chicks in a dish planter, and a ground cover of sedums.*

OPPOSITE, BOTTOM: *Ripe golden yellow fruit of a dwarf citrus create a colour echo with the golden garden in the background.*

– the perfect place for an informal picnic. At the top of the property is a pair of blue metal chairs perched on a white gravel terrace with a bracing view of the ocean – a favourite reading place of the owners. At the end of the gold garden is a curtained pavilion of black trelliswork where Vivien likes to create fresh flower arrangements through the seasons – a perfect spot for formal outdoor dining.

But what really sets Vivien's plant partnerships apart from those of other gardens is their colour echoes – for example, plants with blue foliage, such as *Senecio serpens* (also known as blue chalk sticks), close to a slatted bench of the same hue. As Vivien explains: "It's a simple enough technique, but what makes a colour echo really shine is making sure that there are bold colour contrasts nearby. Many of my favourite colour echoes work well because they involve the purple-leaf form of New Zealand's cabbage tree. It not only has the right chocolate-maroon leaf coloration to highlight paler colour echoes, it has a wonderful explosion of spear-shaped leaves that adds a stimulating textural and sculptural quality to the garden.

When I started gardening here, my mother and I made an English cottage garden as a reminder of places and plants we knew in the old country. But today the garden has evolved into something more original, less demanding of care, with a heavier emphasis on New Zealand native plants than English imports. As a consequence it is much more in harmony with the climate and topography of this part of coastal New Zealand. When visitors come and take a tour they go away feeling they have seen something that is not only beautiful but also unique."

Westridge Garden

Tranquillity in a Hillside Garden

Titirangi is a quiet coastal dormitory suburb on Auckland's west coast, its beaches surrounded by sharp-ridged hills covered in native forest, reminiscent of the coastline around Japan's Inland Sea, complete with misty peaks silhouetting layered tree shapes. Scenes for the film *The Piano* were filmed in the area.

Winding roads lead up from the coast road to beautiful homes set on steep slopes, most with cultivated gardens integrated with the native bush, where they are watered by 150 centimetres of rainfall a year. Up a labyrinth of narrow, zigzag tracks Richard Cadness and Geoffrey Haughey have established a quarter-hectare hillside garden around their home, the result of 25 years of trial and error. Central to the design of their subtropical paradise is a bold flight of flagstone steps they fondly call "the stairway to heaven".

ABOVE: *Close-up of clivia bloom.*
RIGHT: *Stairway ascends a steep slope with shade-loving clivias colonizing the edges.*
INSETS: Brugmansia sanguinea *(top), and* Rhododendron vireya.

Though their first careers – Richard's in ceramic art and Geoff's in architecture – both contributed strongly to the design emphasis on terraces and steps, there was no master plan. It took decades of exhausting weekends working from sunrise to sunset, countless aching backs and constantly empty pockets to thin out the indigenous tree canopy and produce an understorey of exotic plants. "We bought what was a small cottage, in our twenties, and the residence has undergone several major transformations since," says Richard, admiring the home's present modernistic emphasis on large expanses of glass, tubular steel and lofty, minimalist balconies.

One inspiration for the woodland garden was the Rhododendron Dell at Kew Gardens, in England, where Richard and Geoff saw how well rhododendrons flowered beneath a high tree canopy. "Just the solution to underplanting our natural stand of tall tree ferns and nikau palms," recalls Richard. But, after three-quarters of their plantings perished from summer heat, they found only a few kinds of rhododendron were suitable for the site. They took risks with more heat-tolerant exotics, finding many tropicals that would over-winter. These include orange clivias, with umbels of trumpet-shaped blooms, and angel-wing begonias, with sprays of glittering pink flowers. In sunnier areas bromeliads and cymbidium orchids have also been successful.

To Richard and Geoff's surprise their garden became a destination for visiting foreign horticulturists, and they received so many requests for tours they have recently had to curb visits to maintain their privacy. "In 1993, tipped off by Alison McRae, who authored *Gardens to Visit in New Zealand*, we were inundated by New Zealand's 'gang of three'," explains Richard. "In quick succession we admitted garden photographer Gil Hanly, garden writer Julian Matthews and television garden-show host Maggie Barry." The partners still open the garden for a charity event each year, but otherwise prefer to keep a low profile.

Their plant preferences over the years have changed significantly. Whereas flowering effect was once the main objective, they now plant more for foliage and textural contrast. They are especially interested in viewing the garden from the house, through its spacious picture windows, carrying visual interest high into the sky so each window serves as a frame and the view appears to be a painted canvas. The house itself is situated so the living quarters are level with the tops of trees, creating the impression of living in a tree house. To maintain a rainforest aura Richard and Geoff are careful to strike the right balance between tree ferns and nikau palms, liking the way they counterbalance each other, the tree ferns with arching, feathery fronds, the nikau with stiff, erect fronds.

"When we travel we usually choose garden destinations with a particular focus because we are always receptive to ideas," says Geoff. "These have included Holland's Keukenhof Garden, Japan's Imperial Gardens, and even Rio, where we studied the tropical garden designs of the late Roberto Burle Marx. Most recently we broke the garden tour tradition to experience the stark splendour of Antarctica. A breathtaking experience totally unlike anywhere on earth! It made us more acutely aware that there is one addiction we can never give up – the sense of peace and tranquillity of our own green garden."

ABOVE: *View from a balcony of the house showing tops of black mamaku tree ferns and surrounding bush-clad hills.*
RIGHT: *Courtyard between the main house and a guest cottage shows a collection of mostly tropical plants, orchestrated to create a tapestry of foliage contrasts, including a vining rata (centre) and silvery licorice plant used as a ground cover.*

Ayrlies

Auckland's Finest Woodland and Water Garden

Auckland's Mediterranean climate is conducive to making many kinds of gardens, and because the "City of Sails" is New Zealand's most populous city it has an abundance of beautiful private and public gardens. The largest public garden is the Auckland Domain, which features a pair of large conservatories known as the Winter Garden, adjacent to a spectacular outdoor native-fern garden.

Auckland's finest privately owned garden is Ayrlies, a spacious woodland and water garden created by Beverley McConnell and her late husband, Malcolm, on a sunny slope overlooking tidal wetlands bordering the Hauraki Gulf, at Whitford.

ABOVE: *Chinese toon tree* (Cedrela sinensis) *has pink spring foliage.*
RIGHT: *High elevation view of main pond, with bronze-leaf Japanese maple in the foreground and rustic gazebo overlooking the pond.*

46

As Beverley remembers: "We bought the property to run it as a dairy farm, but the undulating, sloping ground and friable soil stimulated my compulsive creative urge to grow a large garden. This resulted first in a hillside garden beside the homestead, then four ponds on a sunny slope. They came about independently, not as a collector's garden or a status symbol, but out of my innate need to produce stimulating effects and to have the air filled with the perfume of flowers."

In the beginning, with five children to raise, it was all Beverley could do to keep her tree plantings watered, but gradually the bones of the garden took shape, and with the children finally grown up she was able to work quickly towards the fulfilment of her dream.

On entering the bowl-shaped entrance garden, the sound of waterfalls draws visitors along meandering paths, over stepping stones that cross narrow water channels, over bridges and around four man-made ponds surrounded by emerald-green lawns. "The garden is intended to evoke a visual adventure, promising an air of tranquillity, and an escape from the pressures of a sometimes noisy, hectic world outside," explains Beverley. "With a series of surprises that unfold as you penetrate deeper into the garden."

What was little more than a bare paddock in 1964 has been transformed into a sanctuary of 15,000 trees, plus myriad choice shrubs, succulents and perennials. Thriving colonies of Japanese and Louisiana irises decorate the pond margins, the Louisianas presenting an astonishing colour range not normally associated with water irises, including ginger and orange. Outcrops of basalt are designed to resemble natural rock ledges, often supporting ground-hugging flowering plants such as silvery sedums and Himalayan knotweed, the latter dipping its crimson flowering stems into the water, like a curtain. The first set of watercourses converges at a cliff-top belvedere that provides a panoramic view of the nearby shoreline.

Just when you think you have completed a satisfying circuit of the garden the path leads through a grove of tall macrocarpas and eucalypts to the contemporary homestead, set into a hill and with the best garden surprises surrounding it. In front of the house is a free-form swimming pool designed

TOP RIGHT: *Agaves, aloes and* Cycas revoluta *with the house in the background.*

CENTRE RIGHT: *Spires of white foxgloves echo the white columns of a temple and white climbing roses.*

BOTTOM RIGHT: *Collection of cycad palms thrive along a dry slope in front of the homestead.*

OPPOSITE: *A series of cascades descend a sunny hillside to a wildlife pond bordered with Louisiana irises.*

ABOVE: *Timbered stairway leads from the bog garden at Ayrlies to a classic temple crowned with rambling roses. The temple is a surprise romantic formal accent in an otherwise informal setting.*
RIGHT: *Like silver threads, a broad cascade of falling water, overhung with native ferns, is one of the three waterfalls feeding a series of sparkling streams that meander downhill to the wildlife pond.*
FAR RIGHT: *Immense planting of orange clivias beneath evergreen redwoods.*

like a desert oasis, surrounded by succulents and drought-tolerant cycad palms planted for their sculptural forms and contrasting leaf textures. Beyond an earth mound sheltering the pool is a hot-colour garden of mostly red, yellow and orange flowers. To step from the cool swimming pool into the hot-colour garden is like entering a sauna.

When once again you think you have come to the garden's limit, a path beckons through more trees to a series of terraces around a fern-fringed water-lily pond, several watercourses spilling downhill towards a rustic gazebo set out over the water. The boggy margins of the pond feature colonies of white arum lilies, blue-leaf hostas, velvety giant gunneras and cheerful bog primulas. A huge colony of 'Green Goddess' arum lilies, with green-tipped spathes, rims a section of pond beside a steep, rocky waterfall, their long, lustrous spear-shaped leaves contrasting with dark bronze-leaf Japanese maples and cone-shaped evergreens. The walk round the pond descends to an even lower level – a woodland garden

that changes from deciduous woodland to evergreen redwoods. Beneath the trees is an immense colony of orange clivias.

At the highest point above the pond is a classic temple atop timbered steps. "Some visitors feel the temple looks a little contrived in such a natural setting," Beverley confides. "But I think it's properly understated and softened with climbing roses and spires of porcelain-white foxgloves. Besides, it reflects my romantic nature – it's like a scene from *A Midsummer Night's Dream*."

Another romantic touch is provided by Beverley's liking for lace-curtain effects, or veiling. This is achieved by training pale-flowering vines into trees, such as 'Wedding Day' roses, white wisteria and *Clematis montana* 'Rubens', and having airy flowers such as white cosmos wave their translucent petals in front of leathery-leaved rhododendrons and camellias.

Beverley has several gardeners to help maintain the property, and considers herself lucky to have been able to engage the services of English landscape designer Oliver Briers in 1972. "Oliver not only shared my vision, he understood how to make the structural components necessary to achieve it." But the exquisite plant partnerships are all Beverley's work – flowers carefully placed like daubs of paint, the earth and sky her canvas, the colours and textures of plants her medium.

LEFT: *Bog garden features several wildlife ponds richly planted with sedge grasses, Japanese bog primulas and white arum lilies.*

53

Noel Scotting's Legacy

Inspiration from a Brazilian Garden Innovator

oberto Burle Marx (1909–94) was a Brazilian artist who created some of the world's most beautiful tropical gardens, many of them for wealthy clients around Rio de Janiero. He also landscaped the famous promenade of Copacabana Beach, and lived not far from Rio in an old *fazenda*, or ranch house, surrounded by banana plantations and rain forest. His style was to use plants in great sweeps, like generous brushstrokes, to "paint" the landscape, not only massing colourful flowers such as drought-resistant yellow day lilies and birds of paradise, but exotic foliage shapes and textures, such as the heart-shaped leaves of taro and the immense circular floating leaves of the Amazon water lily (*Victoria regia*), weaving textures and colour together like a tapestry. He used water generously, often in formal reflecting pools, and some of his hardscape elements, such as arbours and walls, were influenced by Inca architecture.

ABOVE: Canna iridiflora *has pendant, tubular flowers.*
RIGHT: *Native New Zealand nikau palms, with fronds resembling a shuttlecock, make good companions for a giant Brazilian philodendron.*

Not satisfied with the choice of plants available to him, Marx travelled widely, exploring mountains and rivers, bringing into cultivation many plants previously unknown to gardens and propagating them in quantity at a nursery on his property – for example, *Worsleya rayneri*, a blue amaryllis he found in the Carioca Mountains, and the giant bromeliad, *Vriesia imperialis*. His bold, innovative tropical landscapes established his reputation as a skilful designer of exotic gardens on a scale previously unimagined.

Designs inspired by Marx have recently begun to make an appearance in Auckland and Northland, where there are microclimates conducive to growing some of Marx's favourite tropicals. But the late Noel Scotting (1938–97) studied Marx's design style in the 1970s and used his ideas and plant recommendations on her hillside garden near Whitford.

After Noel's death, it took several years to settle her estate, and friends worried that the garden would be lost. But in the summer of 2002 the property was purchased by Auckland florist Jenny Foster, who had the enthusiasm needed to restore the garden. "Never in my wildest dreams did I ever believe I would one day acquire Noel Scotting's legendary garden," says Jenny. "The plants alone would cost a fortune to acquire today, not even taking into consideration the planting and landscaping to accommodate them."

Several plant enthusiasts in the Auckland area feel intimately connected with Noel's garden. Kerry Milne was a gardener there for 25 years, helping Noel propagate and plant thousands of seedlings acquired from tropical areas. She felt so attached to the garden she gave freely of her time to keep it weeded and pruned long after Noel's death. As she says: "Noel's garden is Auckland's best-kept secret. There is nothing like it for its tropical ambiance. The feeling of love and tranquillity is evident immediately, and there is a sensation of profound disbelief at seeing sunny terraces overflowing with exotic plants more reminiscent of a garden in Brazil than New Zealand."

Gillian Walker was a neighbour and close friend of Noel's, and her husband, Graeme, and a contractor, Dave, helped contour the terraces. "On such a steep site they performed miracles. They did ballet with a bulldozer," recalls Kerry.

Another close friend and contributor to the garden is Michael Poulgrain, who Noel considered her best gardening buddy. An active member of the Palm and Cycad Society, he acquired tropical plants and seeds from sources all over the world, allowing Noel to have a fine collection of bromeliads and orchids.

The sense of entering a special plant paradise hits after passing through the entrance gate at the top of the property, with a splendid view of the Hauraki Gulf. From there the

driveway dips steeply through lush tropical vegetation, including giant philodendron vines and aroids with massive heart-shaped leaves. A courtyard at the rear of the homestead is shaded by palms, with grassy paths leading further downhill between a hillside crowded with succulents and a rock garden featuring mature cycads, nikau and washingtonia palms in company with colourful bromeliads and orchids.

A rill of terracotta tiles catches run-off from the hillside garden and directs it to a drainage field, where colonies of cannas and arums testify to the damp soil. The broad curving terrace zigzags downhill under a large arch built from weathered railway ties, emulating the bold, solid lines of the entrance to a ceremonial Inca temple. Healthy colonies of South American crinum lilies and amaryllis mix their trumpet-shaped flowers and straplike leaves with spiny Mexican agaves and South African aloes with poker-like flower clusters.

Pergolas surrounding the house support a rich assortment of flowering vines, framing a small, free-form swimming pool that resembles a rock pool in a jungle clearing, sheltered by palms and a semicircle of tropical foliage.

"Noel was a trick a minute," recalls Gillian. "She became a single mother with four children when her youngest, Sam, was two; yet she managed to buy the property, build a comfortable home, raise her family and develop a magnificent

LEFT: *Timbered arch creates a bold transitional element, separating the gardens surrounding the house from a sunny, secluded terrace with views over the Hauraki Gulf, the edges of the terrace planted with African aloes, Mexican agaves, organ pipe cacti and tropical palms.*

ABOVE: *View of front lawn with free-form swimming pool sheltered by exotic palms, and a pygmy date palm marking the edge of a patio leading off from the main house.*

tropical garden that was the envy of Auckland's gardening elite. She had a soft nature and an infectious sense of humour. I remember going with her to the railway workshops in Auckland to obtain some lumber. We returned with 50 railway sleepers to build steps and terraces, and all they cost was two dozen scones and some good-natured flirting with the railway workers. After that she called me her blonde bombshell."

"If she saw pieces of broken concrete by the side of the road, suitable for pavers, she would stop and load up her little car. Huge boulders for her rockeries appeared like magic. She was always wheeling and dealing and would never accept the first price quoted. She loved a gin and tonic in the garden with friends, opened it to private visits by members of the public, and was featured on one of the early Maggie Barry shows. She started a floristry business when she was just 18, which she gave up to raise her family, but she continued to demonstrate floral art, always using flamboyant plants like palm leaves cut fresh from her garden."

How appropriate that the new owner, Jenny Foster, is herself a professional florist, with a desire to keep the garden's exotic flair and, ultimately, to open it again to private visitation.

PREVIOUS PAGE, LEFT: *A stately nikau palm creates a bold accent at the top of a stairway made from railway sleepers. Subordinate to the nikau are a staghorn fern, African aloes, a cycad and South American bromeliads.*

PREVIOUS PAGE, TOP RIGHT: *Colony of bromeliads and hens-and-chicks decorate a porous rock sheltering the swimming pool.*

PREVIOUS PAGE, BOTTOM RIGHT: *Giant bromeliad,* Vriesia imperialis, *is a trademark of tropical plantings by Roberto Burle Marx, here thriving beside the driveway at the edge of a bamboo grove.*

RIGHT: *A sunny slope overlooking the main driveway is crowded with tropical and sub-tropical plants from around the world, including blue-green* Agave attenuata *(right), spiky African aloes, a handsome African cycad, Brazilian monstera philodendrons and spires of giant echium from the Canary Islands.*

Trelinnoe Park

A Garden Moulded by Man and Earthquake

The great earthquake that destroyed the coastal city of Napier in 1931 raised the coastline by up to two-and-a-half metres. It created high, dry land where previously there had been tidal marshes. The quake's epicentre was at Tutira, in a valley adjacent to the beautiful garden of Trelinnoe Park. Located off the Napier–Taupo road, 46 kilometres from Napier, the garden is set in a landscape whose sharp ridges, rugged hills, deep gullies, steep drop-offs, natural amphitheatres and landslides are evidence of recent earthquake activity. Three hundred metres above sea level, it is part of Trelinnoe Station, established by the Wills family in 1956, and named after a small farm in Cornwall, England, where the present owner's grandfather grew up before emigrating to New Zealand. Coincidentally, the word *trelinnoe* means "glade in the woods", which is an apt description of the garden today.

ABOVE: *Unusual Mexican hand flower* (Chiranthodendron pentadactylon*).*
RIGHT: *Colourful water reflections present a kaleidoscope of colours in early morning light.*

Originally the area was totara forest (*Podocarpus totara*), but this was destroyed in a series of fires, probably set by Maori in the 1700s, following which the land was reclaimed by scrub. In 1956 there was no pasture, stock or buildings – just manuka (*Leptospermum scoparium*) and kanuka (*Kunzea ericoides*) shrubs. Two brothers, Brian and John, progressively worked the station so that today there is a comfortable homestead with outbuildings and grazing for more than 11,000 stock animals.

The garden was begun in 1963 and expanded by degrees to its present size of ten hectares. A person taken there blindfolded from the sumptuous valley garden of Bodnant, in North Wales, might think they were in the same place so similar are the scope of the garden and the extent of its plantings.

OPPOSITE TOP AND BOTTOM: *Early morning shadows sweep across a sloping lawn surrounding the main pond, the waterside jewelled with myriad blossoms of pink azaleas and yellow flag irises.*
ABOVE LEFT: *View from an observation promontory of deciduous and evergreen trees planted to separate the display gardens from native bush. The weeping evergreen in the centre is a blue atlas cedar (Cedrus atlantica 'Glauca Pendula').*
ABOVE RIGHT: *Wooded slope richly planted with fragrant deciduous azaleas, the transluscent foliage of a Japanese maple glowing in the sunlight.*
LEFT: *Flowering specimen cabbage tree displays multiple branches along a woodland path.*

Above all, Trelinnoe is a rhododendron garden, with hundreds of varieties planted along its woodland walks. John and his wife, Fiona, have a special fondness for *Rhododendron nuttallii* because its large, white, trumpet-shaped flowers are highly fragrant and fill the garden with the scent of gardenias when they bloom in mid-October. Numerous mollis azaleas – smaller-flowered cousins of rhododendrons – are also fragrant, and these are planted in bold colour mixtures throughout the garden, their orange, yellow and white blooms mostly edging large expanses of lawn.

All the lawns are free-form in shape, and sloping. Particular attention has been paid to planting the perimeters with tall trees so that in the early morning and late afternoon the sun pencils beautiful shadow patterns across them. A series of ponds separating two large lawn vistas is strategically placed to reflect not only the blue of the sky but also the myriad colours of vibrant flowering and foliage plants crowded around the margins. These include yellow flag irises and blue forget-me-nots, and also a Chinese toon tree (*Cedrela sinensis*) with pink juvenile leaves. As Impressionist painter Claude Monet planted his garden to make exquisite reflections to paint, so the Willses have planted the edges of their ponds to create a stained-glass-window effect on the water's surface, which changes from moment to moment with alterations in the colour of the sky and other atmospheric conditions.

"We are always conscious of the need to make use of the landscape beyond the boundaries of the garden," explains John, "so we have made a number of observation points, keeping the views clear so visitors can look for miles into the surrounding hills. In the woodland we have also worked to produce a number of surprises; for example, people following the main path will suddenly encounter a long curving hedge with evergreens clipped into pyramid shapes, and a large spiralling parterre design planted on a slope. People expect that kind of effect in a sunny space, but not in woodland."

Many trees, such as white birches and paperbark maples, have been planted for their unusual bark coloration, which contrasts with the preponderance of evergreens in the garden. Says Fiona: "I think one of the best times for the garden is May when the autumn leaf display is at its peak. We have a lot of Japanese maples, and few trees give a better autumn display. Also, people don't associate the North Island with good autumn colour."

Floral colour from shrubs and trees abounds in spring and summer, starting early with deciduous magnolias. Frothy pink ornamental cherries, white dogwoods resembling flights of butterflies, Empress paulownias with blue foxglove-like flowers, blue trumpet-flowered jacarandas, and crimson pohutukawa continue to provide colour in the tree canopy

well into summer. A rare Mexican hand-flower tree, billowing to ten metres high, provides a special thrill for children. Known also as devil's claw and monkey paw, its masses of bizarre red flowers emanate from velvety brown sheaths.

In complete contrast to the broad tree-lined avenues and sweeping lawn vistas is a dark, moist, sheltered gully known as the Dell of the Giants. Located next to an arboretum of native trees, the giants include California redwoods, giant Chilean gunneras, towering mamaku tree ferns, tall rimu and giant leathery *Rhododendron sinogrande*, with leaves up to 75 centimetres long.

Each day, after they have closed their tearoom, nursery and craft shop and the visitors have left, the Willses like nothing better than to stroll the garden together, a Jack Russell terrier racing ahead, all three taking in the glory of the garden. "There isn't a day of the year when we cannot find something in bloom, and it never ceases to amaze us how natural it all looks in such a wild setting," John comments with satisfaction.

ABOVE LEFT: *View from a woodland path to a grassy clearing rimmed with azaleas.*
ABOVE CENTRE: *The Great Bowl, an immense natural amphitheatre formed by earthquake activity, rimmed with a rich colour palette of azaleas and rhododendrons.*
ABOVE RIGHT: *Beautiful boxwood parterre creates a labyrinth design on a sunny slope along a woodland path.*
LEFT: *A shaded path with a rustic bench frames a sunny clearing where a dense display of rhododendrons is partnered with a grove of tree ferns.*

Ngamatea

The House in the Tussock

The road from Taihape to Napier is marked on maps as "difficult", a broken line indicating that for 20 kilometres it is unsealed. Most car-rental companies forbid its use, for it is mostly narrow and winding, and forestry trucks hauling lumber, almost as wide as the road itself, barrel along it at regular intervals, stirring up blinding dust.

Before the halfway point the emerald-green hills of sheep pasture are replaced by vast stretches of dry, windswept alpine tussock, resembling a desert. These eventually give way to a series of forested ravines on the descent towards the balmy coast of Hawke's Bay. The desolate midway point, with arid-looking landscape all around, was the location for segments of the popular television series *Xena, Warrior Princess*. Along the banks of the Rangitikei River are to be had some of the best deer-hunting and fly-fishing in New Zealand.

ABOVE: Entrance to one of New Zealand's largest sheep stations where "the house in the tussock" is located.
RIGHT: View from "the house in the tussock" through clumps of various native New Zealand grasses, introduced to create a smooth transition between the modern lines of the house and the expansive natural landscape of red tussock.

Established in 1895, the sheep station Ngamatea (the name has no literal translation) encompasses 32,400 hectares of grazing, has 48,000 sheep, 5500 cattle and 1500 deer, and is at an altitude of 975 metres. It is owned by the late Margaret Apatu's three children – Kathryn, Renata (Ren) and Nathan. Ren took over management of the station on his mother's death. As he explains: "She was a horse woman, from her days as a child, from her days when the property covered 250,000 acres [100,000 hectares]. Everything was done on horseback, with packhorse teams to move supplies. She was a fine woman – featured in Michelle Moir's book *New Zealand Country Women* [Tandem], breeding sport horses and exporting them all over the world."

In 1989 Ren's parents hired a Maori architect, the late John

Scott (famous for the Marist Chapel of Futuna, in Karori) to design a house suitable for the area's harsh climate and in sympathy with the wild landscape. They selected a site on a rise in the heart of the tussock and gave Scott free rein in the design.

In a tribute to Scott, penned for the magazine *NZ House & Garden* shortly after his death, Liz Parker wrote: "His Maori upbringing taught him that the house or building (the *wharenui*) was more than just a shelter for people to live in. It was an expression of their day-to-day life, their future intentions and their history." Parker described Scott as a free-spirited artist who cared little for the tyranny of schedules and bureaucracy yet who designed exquisitely "liveable" houses that have been deeply loved by a succession of owners.

Working with Scott was a labour of love as time was never a factor. Ren recalls his famous line, "The plans will be ready by the end of the month." But he never stated which month he was talking about.

The garden surrounding the house is unobtrusive, containing native plants indigenous to the area. The interaction between residence and garden is the opposite of the usual concept for a garden, where most cultivated plants are introduced. Here the house sits serenely among native vegetation, many of them undisturbed from the time the house foundation was marked out.

ABOVE: *Sheltered from constant winds that sweep across a vast, treeless, alpine plateau, the award-winning house is carefully sited to enjoy breathtaking panoramic views. A collection of New Zealand native shrubs and grasses surrounding the house helps to merge its clean architectural lines with the sea of native red tussock.*

RIGHT: *Panoramic view of the natural landscape surrounding "the house in the tussock", with no human habitation in any direction.*

The native-plants garden covers 13 hectares of fenced tussock, although the transition to the thousands of hectares of pristine subalpine wilderness beyond the fence is imperceptible. While the landscape around the house is mostly red tussock (*Chionochloa rubra*), other indigenous plants have been added for a variety of textures, especially close to the building. A clump of flax provides broad, strap-like leaf shapes, while a colony of toetoe creates an explosion of slender leaves and feathery flower plumes. There are drifts of coral lichen, yellow-flowered spires of Maori onion (*Bulbinella hookeri*) and cushions of the creeping clubmoss *Lycopodium fastigiatum* (a fern ally). Mounds of evergreen hebe are sufficiently wind- and drought-tolerant to produce a welcome dark-green contrast to the predominantly beige coloration and to provide shelter.

"We recognise that the expanse of undulating tussock grassland is the property's most dynamic feature," says Ren, "so we are careful not to interrupt the long, shimmering views and the beautiful shadow patterns that play across it when the sky is filled with scudding clouds. Sunrises and sunsets can be awesome, tinting the tops of the grass leaves as though they are aflame."

A special delight is the autumn flowering of the red tussock around the house, the plants creating a sea of misty, arching, powdery, pollen-laden flower panicles, though this spectacle doesn't take place every year. The grassy terrain is also perfect cover for skylarks. The sound of their melodious song as they climb into the sky seems always present, one bird starting up as another descends.

After the house had been completed John received an Award of Architecture, the citation acknowledging his design's sensitivity to the natural setting. It states: "A house blended into the landscape, the large spreading roof in places seems to bury itself into the rugged landforms. Rich timber finishes are tied with impeccable detail to the unadorned concrete 'bones' of the house. The use of enclosure then openings which give vistas of rolling tussock country, heightens the mystery and anticipation at every turn. Long in the making, this house provides spiritual as well as physical shelter from the frequently harsh climate of Hawke's Bay Hill Country."

Winters are indeed harsh. Ren remembers recently experiencing 60 centimetres of snow for five days. However, with its construction of South African slate, matai panelling, cedar beams and pillars of Corsican pine, the house in the tussock provides a strong sense of security, shutting out the keen winds and biting cold. Equally satisfying is to sweep back the heavy curtains from the huge picture windows and watch the dramatic play of light across the panorama of rolling terrain, from dawn until dusk, unspoiled by any sign of human intrusion.

"The house provides an intense feeling of closeness to nature and a profound sense of solitude, precisely as my parents desired and John Scott intended," says Ren. "Their collaboration produced a unique work of art."

Titoki Point

Gordon Collier's Lasting Legacy

Probably no garden in New Zealand is more celebrated than Gordon Collier's Titoki Point bush garden, near Taihape. It has been made famous by numerous magazine and television features extolling its virtues as a "New Zealand original", and by a book devoted to its history and design integrity covering 30 years of dedication by Gordon and his wife, Annette.

Gordon is well known to New Zealand gardeners, not only as a knowledgeable plantsman, but also as a widely published garden writer. He is now in retirement, and writes about other people's gardens for *NZ House & Garden* and the *New Zealand Gardener*. And although he and Annette have moved to a smaller property in Taupo, the Titoki Point garden, now in the care of Gordon's niece, Pippa, continues to thrill visitors.

ABOVE: *Hens-and-chicks decorate the roof of a mailbox.*
RIGHT: *Overall view of the bog garden from an elevated boardwalk, with the tall straight trunks of California redwoods, creating a high tree canopy that shelters a spectacular collection of hybrid rhododendrons and native tree ferns.*

In full view of Mount Ruapehu, rising out of the tussock-covered volcanic desert between Lake Taupo and Taihape, Titoki Point nestles in a fertile valley of sheep pasture and titoki trees. Though best described as a bush garden on account of the large number of indigenous plants featured, especially cabbage trees and tree ferns (*Cyathea medullaris*), it is a diverse collection of both native and introduced species, the two types complementing each other in a bush setting, thanks to Gordon's skill at spotting unlikely plant partnerships, such as a grove of 80-year-old California redwood trees under-planted with the rengarenga lily (*Arthropodium cirratum*).

"The garden is large and meant to be instantly recognisable as a New Zealand garden," says Gordon, "so I have allowed our trademark native plants, like tree ferns, cabbage trees and lancewoods, to dominate. Small plants tend to get lost in their presence so I have under-planted these natives with bold foliage from ostrich ferns, hostas, ligularias, gunneras and petasites. A third tier of colour comes from more diminutive perennials like bog primulas, snake's head fritillarias and ajugas."

Gordon admits to gardening with an analytical eye. "It's

not just a matter of choosing the right plant for a particular location, but knowing what plants to put together for a visually exciting effect. Also, a garden is always changing, and so it's important to evaluate the overall effect each season, making sure that mass plantings, like arum lilies and agapanthus, stay in the right scale."

After gaining a diploma in horticulture in 1955, Gordon went to London and worked in a high-class nursery in Earl's Court, mostly serving sheltered inner-city gardens, and he saw how New Zealand natives such as tree ferns, hebes, flaxes, manuka and cabbage trees were highly valued. When he returned to New Zealand his ambition was to develop a distinctive garden that he could open to the public. After marrying Annette, he settled on the family farm, Titoki Point, built a house on a high spot, and created a series of interconnected theme gardens between it and the lowest part of a nearby gully.

Around the house itself is a silver garden, featuring the grey *Teucrium fruticans* as a hedge in company with other silvery-grey plants such as phlomises, senecios, astelias, Marlborough daisies and even artichokes.

The garden beyond the house descends steeply to a distant boggy area, with places to pause along its length, such as a roundel enclosed by a circle of camellias with a pedestal at its centre. A long flight of stone steps leads through an avenue of Japanese maples to a pond in a woodland clearing, and a wooden observation deck. At the bottom level, boardwalks cross the bog. The moist soil is threaded with streams, and the sides are planted with arum lilies, bog primulas, forget-me-nots, bronze-leaf flax, blue-leaf hostas and myriad plants with small bright flowers. The embracing slopes feature bolder splashes of colour from billowing rhododendrons and saucer magnolias against a backdrop of towering California redwoods.

Gordon has avoided ostentation, such as ornate statues or fountains. Rather he has introduced structural elements that complement the jungle-like atmosphere, such as a rustic belvedere that provides an elevated view of the bog garden, simple footbridges, and gates made from gnarled totara branches.

The overall effect is so prehistoric-looking one might expect to encounter a dinosaur or a giant moa contentedly eating the tree-fern fronds.

ABOVE: *Native rengarenga lilies (*Arthropodium cirratum*) carpet a woodland slope.*
RIGHT: *Belvedere on stilts provides shelter from rain and a deck gives a view of the bog garden from the tree canopy. Tall, straight trunks of California redwoods rise above the slender, snaking branches of native cabbage trees.*

Rathmoy

A Rangitikei Hill-Country Garden

D r Morgan Stanislaus Grace, born in Ireland and descended from a daughter of William the Conqueror, arrived in Auckland in June 1860. Chief medical officer to the British troops engaged in the New Zealand Wars, at the end of hostilities he chose to settle in the North Island and was moved to write an eyewitness account of the conflict, in a book entitled *A Sketch of the New Zealand War*.

Twenty years before Dr Grace arrived in New Zealand, Scotsman John Duncan had arrived at Port Nicholson (now Wellington) and established one of the largest sheep stations in the country – Otairi – along the Rangitikei River. Otairi encompassed 10,500 hectares of hilly bush, extending 50 kilometres between Hunterville and Taihape. When Jeannie Margaret Duncan, a granddaughter of Duncan's, married George Russell Grace, a grandson of Dr Grace's, two great New Zealand families were united, and the couple established a second sheep station – Rathmoy – east of Otairi.

ABOVE: *Moveable bench utilizing metal cart wheels.*
RIGHT: *View from a downstairs window of the orange garden.*

Today, Rathmoy is the home of George's son, Christopher, and Christopher's wife, Susanna. The couple are not only the owners of Rathmoy, but also share an interest in historic Otairi with other Duncan descendants.

The road to Rathmoy climbs steeply from Hunterville, then levels off at a pair of brick pillars marking the start of a driveway that sweeps onto the property in a great arc, as though encircling an amphitheatre. The approach at first seems formal, with white swans gliding on a pair of man-made lakes. But the formality is soon blurred by an abundance of free-form plantings, and closer to the homestead there is evidence, in the form of several whimsical features, that the owners not only gain a great deal of pleasure from the garden but also have a wonderful sense of humour. The first chuckle comes at the sight of a pair of Wellington boots sticking out of a compost heap; the second when confronted by husband-and-wife scarecrows made from plant pots stacked together, one holding a lawn-mower.

The two-and-a-half-hectare garden is a fraction of Rathmoy's 970 hectares. Susanna maintains the flower gardens while Christopher tends a small vegetable garden, and the two of them share responsibility for a menagerie that includes a family of white fantail doves, flocks of ducks, a llama, stable horses, belted Galloway cattle, a pet mob of sheep and donkeys. The animals live in and around the edges of the garden.

A large, rambunctious black Labrador and a Saint Bernard with doleful eyes and drooling mouth bark fiercely at approaching visitors, but become friendly at Susanna's command.

At 460 metres above sea level, the Graces have a fine view of Mount Ruapehu and were able to enjoy the spectacle of the series of volcanic eruptions in 1995 and 1996. Since the surrounding terrain is mostly hilly sheep pasture, the gardens would be shredded by winds if it were not for tall windbreaks of eucalyptus, karo (*Pittosporum crassifolium*) and Himalayan deodar cedars.

FAR LEFT: *Corner of the bog garden with white arum lilies and white marguerite daisies partnered with fragrant deciduous azaleas.*
TOP LEFT: *An avalanche of white* Clematis montana *cascades from the branches of a eucalyptus tree.*
LEFT: *Overall view of a mixed shrub border that parallels the entrance driveway, showing orange deciduous azaleas and a Japanese pepper tree (*Zanthoxylum piperatum*).*

Susanna's main interest is planting colour harmonies, and no two seasons are the same. The gardens flow one into another in a series of complementary themes. A pastel-coloured area one summer may become all white the next. Susanna also likes mood contrasts: for example, a shady woodland with a bench in a sheltered nook overlooking a sweep of sunlit lawn and glittering blue ponds; or a secluded rose garden with access through the vegetable garden, which has an ornamental character on account of rows of lilies and other cutting flowers rubbing shoulders with silver beet, cabbages and tomatoes. The Graces use a lot of well-decomposed animal manures to feed and mulch the soil.

"If a garden isn't loads of fun, why bother?" is Susanna's credo. "I like to search local sales for old implements and ornaments. Not statues, which remind me of cemeteries, but discarded milk buckets to use as planters and old carts to serve as pedestals for a collection of potted plants."

A rusty tractor wheel placed on a pole above the vegetable garden does duty as a trellis to support red rambler roses and scarlet runner beans, the spokes arching the vines to create a flowering umbrella. Another metal farm wheel has been attached to a bench, allowing the bench to be moved easily from one part of the garden to another.

FAR LEFT: *Whimsical "Bill and Ben" flowerpot scarecrows are a decorative feature of the vegetable garden.*
LEFT: *Dusky pink umbels of* Angelica sylvestris *'Vicar's Mead' thrive beside the lake, where a guest cottage occupies the far shore.*
ABOVE: *Cluster of succulents in containers, chosen for contrasting leaf colours, decorate an outdoor table on the front lawn.*

Over the years the Graces have collected a large quantity of old bricks from abandoned houses, and these they have used in a series of structural embellishments, including a bridge with a Chinese Chippendale pattern modelled after one they saw at Old Basing, England. Bricks have also been used to make paths, a patio for displaying potted plants, and a secluded walled garden which incorporates a dovecote and is entered at one end through a brick arch supporting a climbing rose.

Experiments in colour harmonies abound, those that work being nurtured, the disappointments quickly replaced. Standing before a blue-flowering California lilac (*Ceanothus thyrsiflorus*), its spreading branches weaving through a silvery South African liquorice plant (*Helichrysum petiolare*), Susanna likes the way the blue and silver complement each other and pronounces it a winning combination: "A Susanna original."

"I'm always looking to change plantings to avoid monotony. For example, I like having a white garden, but it's not always in the same place. And I'm always searching for easy-care ways to maintain the garden, like using lots of mulch, six inches deep in places so I don't have to weed. I won't try to change everything at once, but I'm extremely critical of my own work, always dreaming up new plant partnerships for my hydrangeas, wondering where to add more native plants, and making misty effects with silvery plants. In a garden as big as this I can never rest on my laurels,

and I am enthusiastic about visiting other people's gardens."

She is particularly careful to maintain the pioneer spirit of the property. "A fussy Japanese-style garden or an ostentatious Italian baroque garden would be completely out of place here," she insists. "I like people to see Rathmoy as a New Zealand original – sheep on the hillside, Mt Ruapehu snow-capped and sometimes billowing smoke on the horizon, paths that promise a unique visual adventure, the smell of livestock in the pasture, the sound of a pregnant donkey braying contentedly, exotic floral fragrances, and above all my quiet colour harmonies weaving their magic."

ABOVE LEFT: *Vigorous, multi-stemmed hybrid echium rises beside a brick wall dividing the garden from a tennis court.*
ABOVE RIGHT: *Fragrance garden planted in a pink and white theme, includes clumps of David Austin 'Mary Rose' partnered with pink and white varieties of flowering tobacco.*
RIGHT: *View from an upstairs bedroom window of the front lawn with a sitting circle for outdoor entertaining. Judas tree (Cercis siliquastrum), from the Mediterranean, displays a blizzard of rosy-red blossoms.*

Glen Colyn

Magic with Woodland and Water

The agricultural community of Kimbolton is little more than a crossroads with a few short residential streets and a pub, yet it boasts several spectacular gardens. Cross Hills Gardens and the New Zealand Rhododendron Society are well known as world-class rhododendron gardens. Kimbolton's best-kept secret is the magical woodland-and-water garden of Colin Spicer. A retired teacher, Colin has worked single-handedly on a two-and-a-quarter-hectare garden he calls Glen Colyn, preferring the Welsh spelling of his own name to the English. He has also found time to cultivate two satellite gardens, one a shade garden a third of a hectare in area which he calls Westwood, the other a two-thirds-hectare sunny trial garden called Homestead, situated behind his house. The trial garden is where he tests plants for colour and form before deciding whether to place them in one of the other two gardens. Frosts are frequent, and in winter the gardens are often dusted with snow.

ABOVE: *Hellebores in early spring.*
RIGHT: *Bog garden featuring white arum lilies, pink foxgloves and yellow bog primulas.*

Colin is a perfectionist when choosing plants. He is well aware that in the world of horticulture, plants of inferior stock can be sold to the general public. The widespread practice of tissue culture, for example – popular as a means of propagating thousands of hostas quickly from a single parent – can result in weak progeny and off colours. He is so particular about quality he seeks out special selections, propagating only the best colours, sometimes making yet further selections to intensify a particular colour, like the vibrant red he found in a mixed planting of bog primula (*Primula* 'Inshriach Hybrids').

The vigour and vibrancy of the plants is the most striking feature of Colin's gardens; for example, a colony of *Hosta sieboldiana* taller than a person, and an amazing colour mixture of California giant trillium, *Trillium chloropetalum*. This strange-looking woodland plant is mostly seen in one colour – dark red – but scattered about Colin's garden are also pink, maroon, white, cream and yellow specimens, their upright, wavy petals generally much larger than those found in the wild because of his rigorous rejection of anything mediocre or inferior.

When Colin likes a plant's performance, he plants a lot of it – witness a river of yellow *Primula helodoxa* at Glen Colyn and a ribbon of red *Primula pulverulenta* at Westwood. But he is wary of plants that might become invasive. He admires the chocolate-brown leaf coloration of *Ligularia dentata* 'Desdemona' because it combines well with other large-leaf plants such as gunneras, rodgersias, peltyphylums and lysichitons, but he dislikes its tendency aggressively to self-seed in places it isn't welcome, so as soon as it sets its generous, yellow daisy-like flower clusters, he decapitates it in order to prevent it setting viable seed.

Glen Colyn was formerly a paddock, with a farm building in such dilapidated condition Colin had it demolished. On the foundations he created a stone ruin that now serves as a beautiful rockery at the garden's entrance, its brick-shaped stones covered with curtains of vibrant pink soapwort (*Saponaria ocymoides*), white Kaikoura rock daisies (*Pachystegia insignis*) and spreading dwarf yellow Spanish broom. A stream

LEFT: *Blue and variegated hostas, English foxgloves, variegated New Zealand flax and yellow bog primulas make good companions along the edge of a stream.*

TOP RIGHT: *Rustic bridge crosses a small stream where hostas, bog primulas and an umbrella plant (*Peltyphyllum peltatum*) thrive in the moist soil.*

RIGHT: *Grove of soft tree ferns (*Cyathea smithii*) rise above a colony of yellow bog primulas (*Primula helodoxa*) and spires of foxgloves.*

ABOVE: *Stone ruin supports life for a collection of rockery plants, including yellow Spanish broom and pink soapwort (*Saponaria ocymoides*), with 'Inshriach' hybrid bog primulas along the stream bank.*

RIGHT: *Mixture of giant toadshade trilliums (*Trillium chloropetalum*) form a dense ground cover along a woodland path, with a fragrant deciduous azalea in the background.*

flows downhill beside the ruin into a pond rimmed by evergreens, its surface adorned with water lilies. The water flows over a spillway between steeply wooded banks, under a rustic wooden bridge and through a flat boggy section, before leaving the property beyond a grove of white birch and native tree ferns.

A graduate of Massey Agricultural College (now Massey University), Colin spent most of his working life as a tutor of horticultural propagation at Manawatu Polytechnic. His desire to cultivate an outstanding garden grew out of a visit to Eastwoodhill Arboretum, near Gisborne. The founder, the late Douglas Cook, was a serious collector of mostly woody plants,

and Colin remembers thinking he could do something similar on a smaller scale. As a result he purchased Glen Colyn in 1964, Westwood in 1968 and his retirement home in 1993.

Colin likes to grow plants from seed, corresponding with seedsmen in Scotland and Japan for many of his best stocks. He has a special fondness for witch hazels and camellias, for these are the first to bloom as spring approaches, even before the last snowfalls of winter. He deplores the spread of camellia blight, a disease unknown in New Zealand until it was recently discovered infecting plants in Wellington's Botanic Garden. "Some idiot must have brought in some diseased flowers from abroad," he laments, "so now the entire country is infected with it, and it will require the breeding of a whole new race of disease-resistant plants to make camellias worth growing again."

Hellebores are another favourite for their early bloom, but he scoffs at the attempts of breeders to make them erect-flowering. "They look so unnatural that way," he opines. "It's much better to have the blooms stay pendant and to grow them as a slope cover so they can be viewed from below." He is currently working on a special red-flowered strain. He has also turned his attention to *Rhodohypoxis*, a South African alpine plant that produces masses of star-shaped flowers in mostly white, pink and red. He has not only succeeded in raising plants with more than one row of petals, but also bicoloured specimens, striped like a candy cane, that flower for seven to eight weeks.

Visitors to Glen Colyn marvel at so much space cultivated by one person. He ascribes his success to strong emotional support from his wife, June, and a maintenance system he calls "horticultural technology", which utilises both ancient and modern methods of weed control, including using leaf mould as a mulch among beds, leaving prunings beneath woody plants in woodland areas, and applying a selective herbicidal spray on grassy areas.

"A woodland garden doesn't have to be a fussy garden," he adds pragmatically. "And in shady areas weeds aren't as aggressive as in sunlight. Also, nobody minds an occasional brush pile or leaf pile quietly decomposing among the leaf litter. Besides, they are good places for some of my Himalayan cardiocrinum lilies and California trilliums to self-sow and start a new colony. It's always a special thrill when that happens."

LEFT: *Narrow stream with railway sleepers to slow the flow of water, is planted along its length with masses of moisture-loving plants, such as 'Inshriach' hybrid bog primulas, hostas, astilbe and Japanese iris.*

Cross Hills

Two Thousand Rhododendrons and an Avalanche of Clematis

When the late Eric Wilson retired from farming in the late 1960s and handed the reins to his two sons, Rodney and Graham, he looked for an activity that would make his retirement years productive. So he started a garden, turning paddocks and an orchard near the house into terraces to accommodate trees and shrubs. It was the beginning of a world-class rhododendron garden.

Named after a suburb of Aberdeen, Scotland, where Eric's grandfather used to live, Cross Hills began as a farm in 1886 when the area was virgin bush.

ABOVE: *Hybrid rhododendron 'Lemon Lodge'.*
RIGHT: *Sparkling waterfalls descend a steep hillside to create a series of small ponds richly planted with Japanese cut-leaf maples, tree ferns and native kowhai trees* (Sophora microphylla), *with yellow flowers.*

The first settler built a modest homestead close to the main road between Palmerston North and Taupo, surrounding it with macrocarpas for shelter. Two of the massive trees remain, along with a 100-year-old oak. The 240-hectare property prospered as a sheep and cattle station, all its timbered structures built of macrocarpa milled on site. Stones hand-selected from the foothills of the Ruahine Range were also used for construction, and stones of the same kind subsequently went into walls and terraces throughout the garden.

Following the building of a new homestead in 1951, the grounds were landscaped with native and exotic plants, including rhododendrons, which proved especially free-flowering, liking as they did the area's acid soil, sharp winters and regular rainfall.

Wherever the soil was thin or impoverished, tonnes of topsoil were spread to form mounds and beds for planting a diverse assortment of trees to shade the rhododendrons. A trickle of visitors saw knowledge of the garden gradually spread by word of mouth, so a decision was made to open it to the public, with a nursery to help pay for overheads, the proceeds enabling it to reach its present size of seven hectares.

At first, the Wilsons concentrated on making a garden of mostly woody plants, because these were enduring and required little care compared with herbaceous plants like annuals and perennials. But in 1990 a bold departure was attempted in the form of an ambitious water garden fed by a series of waterfalls, beneath a bank cloaked in three varieties of *Clematis montana*. These bloom white and pink at the same time as the peak flowering of the rhododendrons, of which there are now more than 2000. Most years this event coincides with the kowhai blossom, the canary-yellow flowers harmonising with drifts of blue forget-me-nots and yellow bog primulas.

The main inspiration behind the creation of such a lavish rhododendron display was an overseas trip Eric and his wife, Merle, took in 1969, visiting famous gardens in England, France and North America. The Butchart Gardens, on Vancouver Island, proved the most motivational.

Eric's younger son, Rodney, and his wife, Faith, took over full-time management of Cross Hills and the adjoining nursery in 1981, and worked steadfastly to make it an all-seasons garden, so when the main rhododendron display fades at Christmas, it is now followed by yet more floral colour, from summer perennials, cardiocrinum lilies, roses, hydrangeas, garden lilies and dahlias. Along paths that loop back and forth along three main levels, visitors also encounter a tree-peony glade, a camellia maze and a conifer valley. The garden enjoys spectacular autumn hues from maples, liquidambars and other deciduous trees, the colour peaking in May.

Rodney feels that the bones of Cross Hills are now well established, and the majority of rhododendrons have reached a fine maturity, so he wants to concentrate on fine-tuning the plantings and to improve promotion to encourage more visitors. As he explains: "Kimbolton is off the main tourist route, and so we have to make an extra effort to draw visitors. What I would like to see for the future is a world tour of great gardens sponsored by the tourist offices of the various gardening nations, with Cross Hills on the list of great New Zealand gardens to visit. After seeing all the other countries, tourists would then realise that we are the greatest gardening nation on earth."

ABOVE LEFT: *Line of rhododendron standards trained to a single trunk, viewed from the top of the clematis bank.*

TOP RIGHT: *The clematis bank with three varieties of* Clematis montana, *mingling their blossoms. A spectacular specimen of native kowhai tree glows bright yellow in the foreground.*

BOTTOM RIGHT: *Overall view of pools showing a line of tree-form pink rhododendrons overhung by a weeping willow in the background.*

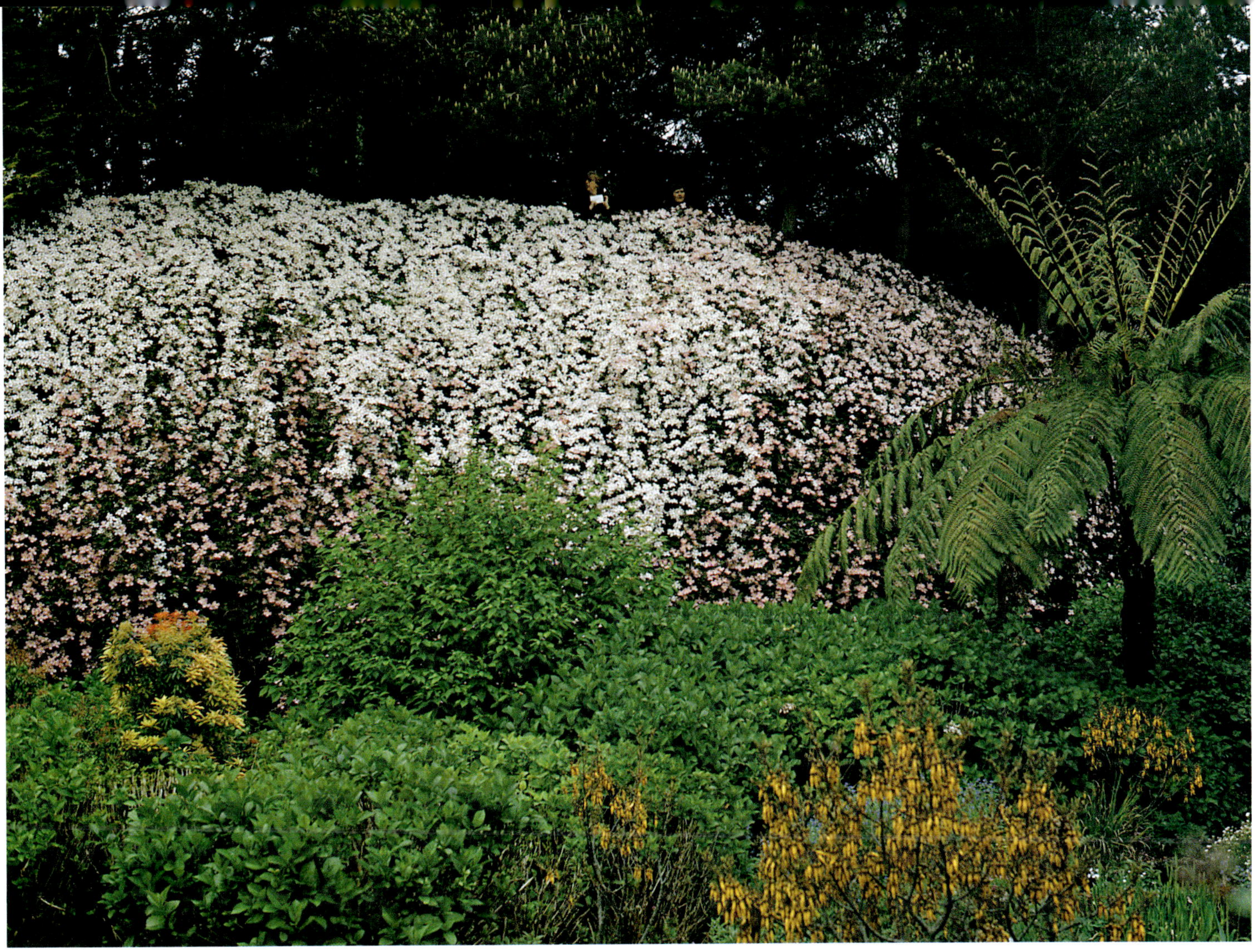

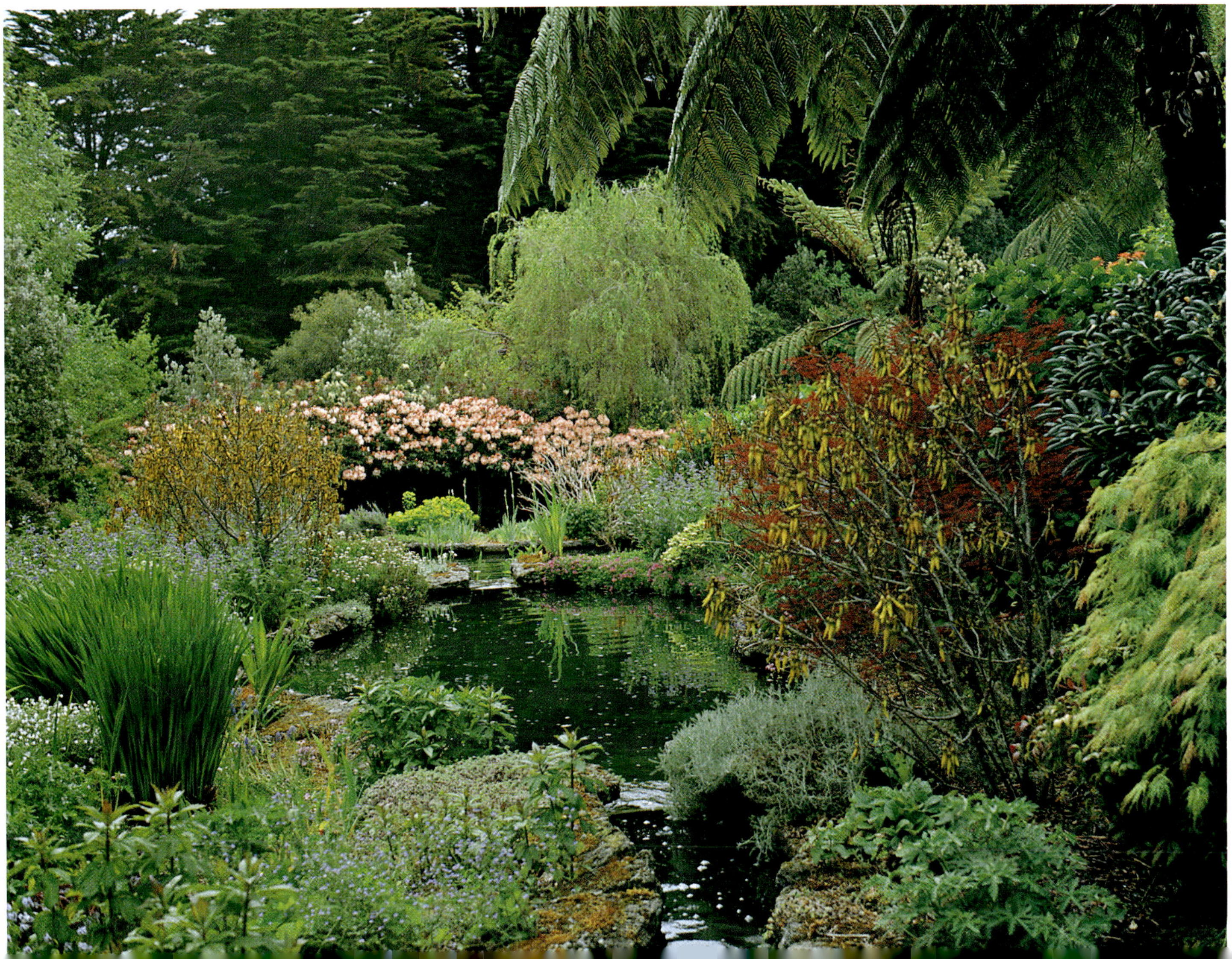

Pukemarama

A Hillside Garden with Moonlight Walks

*P*ukemarama (the name means "moon-viewing hill") is a beautiful colonial homestead built on a stabilised sand hill near Palmerston North. Beyond the front door, below a veranda covered in roses and bougainvillea, is a spectacular formal garden with a strong central axis that provides views over the lower Rangitikei Plain. The wide Victorian house dominates the hill, which is ascended by an entrance path via a series of wide brick terraces along an imposing cement stairway, so that the view looking up is as imposing as the view looking down. From the rear of the house, looking west, there are views to the Kapiti Coast, with Kapiti Island itself visible on a clear day.

ABOVE: *Maiden statue in the perennial garden.*
RIGHT: *Main house and garden terraces in early summer, planted in a mostly pink and red colour theme.*

Looking south from the top floor, it is possible to see the snow-capped mountains of the South Island's Kaikoura Range, and to the north-west the snow-covered peak of Mount Taranaki.

The house and garden date back to 1900, when the late James McKelvie hired a firm of local architects, Russell & Gilmore, to design the house, and a landscape architect by the name of Agate to lay out the garden. A prominent local nursery, Harrison Nurseries, was then commissioned to surround the property with a spectacular assortment of trees. Some of these have since had to be removed to maintain the

ABOVE LEFT: *Top terrace with ivy-leaf geraniums and blue convolvulus spilling over the retaining wall.*
ABOVE TOP RIGHT: *Summery pink and red colour harmony from mostly roses, sweet William and nicotiana.*
ABOVE BOTTOM RIGHT: *Spectacular weeping beech is a feature of the lower lawn.*
LEFT: *Rhododendrons shelter part of the front porch.*
RIGHT: *Spent petals of a camellia carpet a path that encircles the lower garden. The backlit foliage of a weeping beech lights up the background.*

views, but many have reached a maturity few other New Zealand gardens can boast, their placement perfectly in scale with the spaciousness of the garden. Of particular note are a majestic weeping cherry and a wide-spreading weeping beech that elegantly frame a roomy bottle-green summerhouse beside an encircling path. Moreover, the distinctive Victorian architecture of the homestead, and the long steep flight of steps, reminiscent of Tuscany gardens, combine to make the garden look much older than it really is.

The garden is the special pride of Sue McKelvie, who freely admits to using it to indulge her romantic personality, recently surprising her husband, Ian, by planting 90 fragrant 'Dublin Bay' roses ("His favourite variety") along a newly erected trellised boundary fence. As she confides: "As long as I plant lots of red in the garden Ian will let me have anything. We have raised three children, and when we came to live here the place was a shambles. There was so much lawn to cut and so many trees to prune we felt almost overwhelmed, and couldn't rush anything."

Now, with the garden restored, Sue orchestrates a harmony of romantic tones in the flowerbeds by using predominantly pastel colours, especially shades of blue and pink. She likes harmonious mixtures of old-fashioned plants such as sweet William, lilies and foxgloves, but dislikes orange except in autumn, when many of the deciduous trees turn shades of russet.

"Recently I've gone mad on tall bearded irises," she says. "They're beautiful displayed in vases, they have a pleasant peppery fragrance, and the wide colour range can produce a striking rainbow effect. Fragrance is very important to me. Walking the terraces at night the scent is especially noticeable. Also, I have added lights to the garden so visitors can enjoy its charms at night. With lights illuminating the pathways, and opera music carrying from the house into the garden, it's just magical."

The garden's clean, bold design and flower-filled terraces are beautiful, but it is the adjacent copse of trees that awes many visitors. Reminiscent of old Scottish estates, the woodland hides a sweeping gravel driveway that curves discretely uphill, revealing the homestead at the last moment and providing an elevated view of 100-year-old English oaks, macrocarpas, Norfolk Island pines and Chinese fan palms, the sturdy forms of these magnificent trees soaring above an under-storey of rhododendrons, azaleas and camellias.

On a moonlit night a walk through the woodland is like entering the world of Tolkien, for the trees not only have near-human characteristics, their wide-spreading limbs and tracery of branch silhouettes pencil-delicate moon shadows over the woodland floor and across the greensward.

LEFT: *Massive trunk of a century-old Norfolk Island pine towers above the lower lawn.*
TOP: *Bridge crosses a boggy area with a beautiful specimen Chinese fan palm displaying powdery yellow flower clusters.*
ABOVE: *French lavender in peak bloom lines one of the terraces.*

Ngamamaku

On the Slopes of Mount Taranaki

The area around New Plymouth, in the shadow of Mount Taranaki, is famous for several fierce battles during the New Zealand Wars. One of these, near Oakura, resulted in a defeat for the British known as the Ahuahu Massacre. A large number of British were killed when Maori duped a mixed army of soldiers and sailors into attacking a pa in the belief that it was occupied by the main Maori force. After they had reduced the pa to splinters with artillery and then stormed it, the British found it mostly empty. The main body of Maori was in fact entrenched on a nearby hillside, a tactical ploy that allowed their sharpshooters to pick off the exposed British.

ABOVE: *Easter Island statue decorates part of a bush walk.*
RIGHT: *View looking uphill from the bog garden, with a vigorous clump of 'Green Goddess' arum lilies in the foreground.*

An historic-trail marker along the coast road directs visitors to the site of the battle, adjacent to a beautiful garden that integrates bush-clad slopes and a cascading rocky stream with both natural and formal settings that are the work of partners Tony Barnes and John Sole.

Tony gained an intimate knowledge of plants while working for one of New Zealand's leading nurseries, Duncan and Davies, where he supervised export-packing and the propagation of mostly ornamental shrubs, especially maples and conifers. Seventeen years' service was followed by three years working for Egmont Roses, after which he joined Matthew Roses, his present employer. Tony's familiarity with plants means he is responsible for plantings while John takes care of garden maintenance.

Ngamamaku means "place of the tree ferns", and groves of silver tree fern (*Cyathea dealbata*) cover the hillside, with an occasional nikau palm striking through the canopy. Little else was in place when Tony and John purchased the property in 1986, but it had obvious potential, being sheltered and secluded. They began at the driveway entrance and gradually worked their way up a ravine known locally as Lucy's Gully, using the stream to link what became a series of theme gardens on several levels.

The edges of the stream are planted as a bog garden, with moisture-loving perennials such as bog primulas, yellow skunk cabbage and flag irises thriving along its course. Higher up the banks, a verdant fringe of Japanese maples combines with azaleas, camellias and magnolias in merging with the native bush.

A formal paved circle on one of the lower levels marks the site of a rose garden planted as a memorial to John's mother. It features a maiden statue in the middle, a circle of boxwood hedging and an outer perimeter of ponga trunks that form a sunny rose-covered pergola, the spaces between the roses vibrant with English perennials such as foxgloves and hellebores.

Between the rose garden and a pond at the top of the property is a dense area of natural bush, with paths cut through it criss-crossing the stream. The tree canopy is filled with bird song and the whoosh of New Zealand pigeons as they fly from one roost to another. A surprise element beside the path is a scaled-down replica of an Easter Island statue. The pond itself shimmers in a clearing with views out to the Tasman Sea, the margins repeating some of the bog plants from the lower reaches of the stream to create colourful echoes and reflections.

The almost three hectares of garden nestle under a spur of the Kaitake Range, well protected from both the southerlies and northerlies that sweep up and down the coast, its cup-

shaped situation capturing the sun. Even so, the garden has suffered set-backs, including devastation by Cyclone Bola in 1988, when the stream became a raging torrent, silting up every level and uprooting everything in its path. "But we employed a digger to clear the debris," John remembers, "and 18 months later you could hardly tell we had been obliterated by flood the regeneration of plants was so rapid."

Thirty minutes' drive inland, towards Mount Taranaki, is the famous Pukeiti Rhododendron Trust, inspiration of the Taranaki Rhododendron Festival, held at the end of October each year. Since 1990 Ngamamaku has been one of the festival's featured gardens, local volunteers setting up a tea tent and welcoming up to 6000 visitors.

"It's a wonderful way to share the garden," says John. "And we meet lots of interesting people, even visitors from foreign countries. A favourite topic of discussion is how best New Zealanders can create distinctive gardens. If you have natives on your property, they can be highlighted and non-natives introduced for embellishment, but subordinate to the natives. That's one way to do it, and it's worked for us. It's labour-saving, too, because when you let the wild plants remain, the garden requires less care except for grooming."

A pavilion next to the house features a velvet rectangular bowling green and topiary figures fashioned out of Virginia junipers and weeping honey locusts in sunken concrete tubs, the junipers' evergreen branches shaped into perfect spheres and pyramids. "It's my favourite area, though most visitors hardly give it a glance," Tony confesses. "I suppose they think something so clean, open and regimented looks out of place here."

ABOVE LEFT: *Hostas and bog primulas edge the wildlife pond.*
TOP: *Overall view of wildlife pond with Japanese hakone grass.*
FAR LEFT: *Topiary junipers and weeping honey locust.*
LEFT: *Flower girl statue among perennial geraniums and foxgloves.*

Burnard Gardens

Englishness and Native Bush in Waikanae

In the history of New Zealand gardening two energetic women stand out for their contributions to the appreciation of the country's gardens. They are Mary Burnard, who authored the first book about private gardens in New Zealand, and Alison McRae, author of the first comprehensive list of gardens open to the public. Mary's book, entitled *Garden Heritage of New Zealand*, features her own photography, and she published it herself in 1984. In 1990 she followed up with a second book, called *The New Garden Heritage of New Zealand*.

Mary describes herself as a "mad-keen" gardener. She loves visiting other people's gardens, and has lavished an enormous amount of time and expense developing a distinctive garden of her own.

ABOVE: *Cardiocrinum lily's trumpet shaped blooms.*
RIGHT: *Classical Tuscan-style tiered fountain surrounded by French lavender and annual corn poppies.*

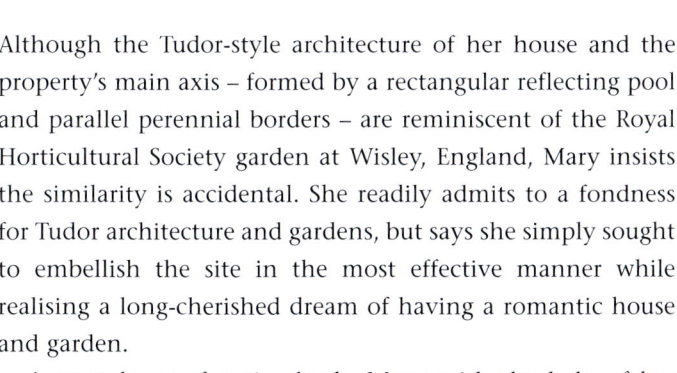

Although the Tudor-style architecture of her house and the property's main axis – formed by a rectangular reflecting pool and parallel perennial borders – are reminiscent of the Royal Horticultural Society garden at Wisley, England, Mary insists the similarity is accidental. She readily admits to a fondness for Tudor architecture and gardens, but says she simply sought to embellish the site in the most effective manner while realising a long-cherished dream of having a romantic house and garden.

A great lover of native bush, Mary, with the help of her husband, Robert, has established a walk for enjoying the local indigenous plant life, going so far as to cut trails down to the Waikanae River so the bush can be viewed from clearings along the way and from several wide pebble beaches.

Mary was born in South Africa and emigrated to New Zealand in 1950 with her Dutch parents and two brothers. She spent her childhood in Rotorua, where her father worked for the Forest Research Institute. She and Robert – a Wellington lawyer – married in 1970 and went on to raise two daughters. They purchased the Waikanae property in 1982 after answering a newspaper advertisement that described the land as 'four hectares of paradise'. Says Mary: "It was no

OPPOSITE: *View of native bush across the Waikanae River from the Burnards' bush walk.*

TOP LEFT: *Native kiekie vine with observation lookout and bench to contemplate its splendour.*

TOP RIGHT: *Herb garden featuring corn poppies and regal lily for decorative effect.*

ABOVE: *Fantail doves taking a bath.*

exaggeration. Previously pastureland grazed by sheep and cattle, it was situated inland from Waikanae along the Akatarawa Road at a place Maori called Reikorangi, meaning 'pathway to heaven'. Located between sheltering hills, it was, I immediately realised, the perfect setting for my dream garden."

A row of closely spaced Leyland cypresses, planted along the exposed sections of the property's boundary, quickly formed a sheltering hedge. After the house had been built, facing north, Mary established the central axis of formal water-lily pool and twin perennial borders 60 metres long and four metres wide. The borders came first. To avoid a hodgepodge of colour, Mary planted them in a series of separate colour blocks that formed harmonies advocated by Gertrude Jekyll. "At both ends there is yellow with a touch of orange," she points out. "Next to this, pure blue. The colouring then passes through the colours of the rainbow – pink, lavender, purple and red."

The borders in place, Mary sited the pool, setting it in a sunken area. It is home to 14 varieties of hardy water lily, of which her favourites are two deep reds, 'Escarboucle' and 'James Brydon', both developed by a French nurseryman around 1900 and featured in the restored water garden of Impressionist painter Claude Monet.

A cross axis leads through tall cypress hedges on the east side to a formal garden with boxwood parterres, and a central gazebo with an elevated view of the parterre design. A gap in the hedge provides access to a formal fountain garden, designed to complement a pavilion where special functions and wedding receptions can be held. From here a path leads to a kitchen garden, which includes a herb garden, orchard and potager.

Mary likes visitors to follow the bush trail as the finale to their enjoyment of the property. Its entire length is kept free of cultivated plants so native ferns, mosses and orchids can flourish beneath the canopy of native trees and vines. A grove of mature toothed lancewoods (*Pseudopanax ferox*) and an unusually tall kiekie vine (*Freycinetia banksii*) are highlights. A full view of the kiekie can be had from an observation platform and bench on the opposite riverbank.

The lancewood grove, at the start of the trail, includes juveniles as well as several mature specimens, making it easy to see why this tree is considered one of New Zealand's most remarkable. In its juvenile stage its trunk shoots straight up like a broomstick, with slender, tough, toothed leaves pointing downwards. On reaching a height of about three metres, however, it sheds its lower leaves, leaving a polished trunk, and develops a bushy topknot of shorter, wider leaves. Botanists theorise that over millions of years of being browsed

by moa, the lancewood developed this particular growth habit as a protective strategy.

Summing up her enjoyment of the garden today, Mary says: "One of my earliest desires was to live in the country in a cosy cottage garlanded with fragrant honeysuckle and roses. I am fortunate to be able to share this cherished dream with a supportive husband and two beautiful daughters. That's what makes it all worthwhile."

LEFT: *View along the bush walk of a native kiekie vine* (Freycinetia banksii) *and a native tree fern.*
TOP: *Main house from perennial garden.*
ABOVE: *View of formal reflecting pool from the balcony of the main house.*

Moss Green

A Hidden World on the Akatarawa River

When visitors to Moss Green make the turn onto Akatarawa Road, in Lower Hutt, the wilderness seems intimidating, especially on those mornings when mist lingers in the hollows. For kilometre after tortuous kilometre the narrow road twists and winds, dips and rises through thick forest, following the Akatarawa River. There are few signs of human habitation. Steep cliffs keep the road in almost perpetual shadow, slips frequently reduce passage to a single car's width, and just as a feeling of being lost starts to take over, a tiny sign on a telephone pole says "Moss Green Garden, 7 km ahead".

Expectations of finding a beautiful garden look set for disappointment when a second sign points down a gravel driveway so dark and shaded there seems insufficient light to grow anything but ferns and mosses.

ABOVE: *Main house from entrance driveway.*
RIGHT: *Bog garden with bog primulas and Japanese water iris in the foreground, and bold clumps of variegated miscanthus and dark green quills of New Zealand jointed rush in the background.*

Then, ahead, an oasis of light appears, and a long swath of *Hosta plantaginea* with thick, heavily veined leaves, each plant spreading two metres wide. Beyond, a tall prickly clump of gunneras fans out huge, ruffled leaves, and clusters of yellow and pink candelabra primulas shine like glow-worms in its shadow.

Further ahead still, a vigorous, sun-loving clump of toetoe beckons, and silvery stands of tall thistle-like cardoon frame a rustic two-storey house with a red corrugated roof, yellow Welsh poppies dancing among clumps of New Zealand carex sedge. Rambling roses scramble over a porch keeping stacks of firewood dry, and the sound of rippling water is amplified by steep riverbanks billowing with rimu and tree ferns.

It took a lot of faith to believe such a wild place could be tamed, but to Bob and Jo Monro, both born in England, it was a challenge they felt ready to accept. Seeking a self-sufficient lifestyle, they purchased the raw land in 1970 and began hacking out a paddock, clearing mountains of gorse, bracken and tangled bush. Beside the river they levelled a boulder-strewn site for a homestead, which Bob built himself single-handed.

The garden was started before the house, and the saga of its creation has been told by Jo in five chapters spanning five issues of Britain's prestigious gardening magazine *Hortus*. The story is a buoyant narrative full of good humour, interesting anecdotes and descriptive prose that often reads like poetry as it tells its tale of triumph over adversity.

Jo and Bob were potters when they purchased the land, but when the pottery market became glutted they turned to operating a plant nursery, and then, in 1990, they opened their garden to the public. The only area suitable for cultivation was a flood plain in an elbow of the river, now out of harm's way because the water cuts such a deep channel.

After clearing the 16-hectare site of bush, Jo and Bob had to contend with mountains of rocks. Some they used for the house foundations, others to make walls, seats and sculptures,

but most went into the creation of raised beds filled with rich compost. The biggest boulders were placed strategically around the garden as decorative accents, while smaller, flat ones served as stepping-stones. Rainfall is high – 275 centimetres a year – frosts are common in winter and the rate of decomposition is high. "Where the soil isn't stony," says Jo, "it's a grey, impervious clay, and in need of so much humus it's the amount of compost available that limits what we can do. The garden is voracious in its appetite for compost – it's like feeding a living creature."

The only way to tame the land was to work with its natural topography, locating swampy areas to make bog gardens for flag irises, bog primulas and astilbes, and identifying areas with good drainage for plants susceptible to root rot, such as roses and vegetables. Strict formality was out of the question.

The garden had to be one that didn't try to assert itself among the native bush, rather wove a tapestry compatible with indigenous plants. One boggy area was excavated to make a pond edged with tree ferns and sedges.

The most recent venture is a fern garden, set against a hillside, featuring mostly New Zealand natives. Jo and Bob's favourite is the black tree fern, *Cyathea medullaris*, the largest of New Zealand's tree ferns. Its trunk can grow to 15 metres tall and its fronds to six metres across. A colony of these has a rich under-planting of crown fern, *Blechnum discolor*, valued for its light-green, translucent, fishbone-shaped fronds in spring and its dark fronds when mature. Says Jo, writing in *Hortus*: "I realise now that my favourite colours in the garden are associated with leaves rather than flowers, especially when the sun is low and provides backlighting. My favourite times

are dawn and dusk . . . There is something magical about morning light in summer. Dew casts a gossamer shawl of the softest grey over everything . . . Then the shadows deepen, until that moment when a shaft of sunlight pierces the trees . . . In the evening, when the light is almost gone, some colours glow like Chinese lanterns in the fading light."

Fragrance is important to the Monros, and plants noted for alluring scents abound. "Trimming and cutting back rampant growth is an enjoyable task when it is accompanied by the spicy fragrance of lavender, and the pungent smells of catmint, wormwood, yarrow and nasturtiums," says Jo. Another of her favourite places is the river walk in summer, when the scent of pine and eucalyptus resin pervades the air. The path leads to a crystal-clear swimming hole, deep enough to jump in and submerge oneself in the cold, invigorating water. "The water has a clean bush smell," says Jo. "When I get out my skin tingles. I walk back over the warm stones and cushions of springy *Raoulia*, up the steep bank and into the garden. I feel revived and rejuvenated after a long day, and no matter how little money we earn, I marvel at how wealthy I feel."

ABOVE FAR LEFT: *Vigorous mass planting of hostas greets visitors at the garden entrance.*
LEFT: *Leafy tunnel formed by rhododendron branches, with spent blossoms carpeting the path.*
ABOVE: *Plank bridge crosses a corner of the pond with* Lysichiton *foliage spilling into the path.*

South Island GARDENS

THE SOUTHERN ALPS catch the prevailing westerly winds and cause high rainfall throughout Westland, creating rainforests filled with luxuriant mosses and ferns, and temperatures are cool even in summer. The area is sparsely populated, with little industry, so gardens along the West Coast tend to be food gardens for supporting a self-sufficient style of living. The more populous east coast generally has warm, dry summers and cool, frosty winters, with many flower gardens concentrated around the cities of Christchurch and Dunedin. Christchurch, the "garden city", attracted mostly English families during its early settlement, while Dunedin is where many Scottish immigrants settled. Gardens tend to feature a large number of temperate plants, especially roses, hardy perennials and rhododendrons. Two emblematic South Island plant species are the Mount Cook lily, or mountain buttercup (*Ranunculus lyallii*), which grows in alpine meadows, and the Southern rata (*Metrosideros umbellata*), particularly common in the forested gorge-like valleys west of the Main Divide and on Stewart Island. More common than either, however, is the Russell lupin, a hybrid of North American lupin varieties developed in England and now considered the South Island's most invasive plant species. Its multicoloured flower spikes are prolific along waysides, especially in Central Otago, and in dry riverbeds, nowhere more so than around the entrance to Arthur's Pass.

LEFT: *Russell lupins naturalised at Arthur's Pass.*

Winterhome

Bold Formality along the Kaikoura Coast

W
hen tourists cross from the North to the South Island, they invariably fly from Wellington to Christchurch, which is a shame, for in not taking the ferry from Wellington to Picton, they miss the scenic waterway of Tory Channel and the upper section of Queen Charlotte Sound.

To drive from Picton to Christchurch there is a choice between State Highway 1, which follows the east coast directly south, and the road west to Nelson and either Lewis or Arthur's Pass. It's a difficult choice, for both routes are scenic, but Highway 1 is quicker and allows a visit to the historic whaling town of Kaikoura and its rocky coastline crowded with fur seals and teeming with seabirds. Just south of Seddon the road runs for miles beside colonies of one of New Zealand's most treasured perennial wild flowers, the Marlborough rock daisy (*Pachystegia insignis*), which grows in clumps in the shaly terrain, displaying silvery, lancelike leaves and white-petalled, yellow-eyed flowers.

About midway between Blenheim and Kaikoura is the tiny coastal community of Kekerengu, with a craft store and restaurant run by Richard and Susan Mcfarlane. The Mcfarlanes live nearby, and have an unusual coastal garden, where an amazing transformation has taken place over a period of less than 20 years.

"The land around Winterhome was first settled by my Canadian grandfather, Commander Sandford Critchley," says Susan. "He was a retired naval officer, artist and farmer, and named the property after the family's estate in Ottawa."

Commander Critchley's discerning eye recognised a cliff-top pasture surrounded by pine trees as a perfect spot to build a home, and moved a cottage from another part of Marlborough to the site. He then engaged architect Heathcote Helmore to expand the cottage. Quick-growing pine, macrocarpa and gum trees were planted for shelter, and a modest garden was started, with stunning views of the Pacific Ocean.

"We came to the property in 1975," recalls Susan. "And our first attempts at expanding the gardens were thwarted by extreme climatic conditions, particularly drought and destruction wrought by Cyclone Allison. Then, in 1980, we hired Sir Miles Warren, owner of Ohinetahi, Governor's Bay [see page 138], to plan some major additions to the house, and his enthusiasm for formal gardens inspired us to plan a series of them, with a strong axis running north towards the Kaikoura mountains."

The main axis begins at a reflecting pool filled with water lilies, and continues along a grass path between facing perennial borders. A second axis, parallel to the main one, begins at the veranda and crosses a greensward between rose beds and perennial borders to a Lutyens-style teak bench. Brick patios, brick walls, a brick-edged swimming pool and a brick-pillared pergola are additional formal features, the walls softened by espaliered apple trees and the pergola by climbing roses and flowering vines. There is an avocado orchard in a

PREVIOUS PAGE TOP LEFT: *Boxwood parterres in a woodland glade, with echiums backlit by the afternoon sun.*

PREVIOUS PAGE RIGHT: *Clifftop view of the Pacific through the branches of two European olive trees that help to shelter the homestead from coastal winds.*

LEFT: *Formal reflecting pool, designed by Christchurch architect Sir Miles Warren, features mostly pink roses to echo the colour of the brick.*

TOP RIGHT: *Circular driveway with beds of agapanthus and the end wall to the reflecting pool, its top garlanded with roses.*

BOTTOM RIGHT: *Historic homestead with raised water lily pool.*

cliff-top meadow reached via a suspension bridge, and an orange orchard in a parterre garden beside the driveway where it sweeps in a wide arc towards the homestead.

A favourite time for the Mcfarlanes to walk the garden is late afternoon, when the sun sinks low over the mountains and beautiful shadow patterns, especially from the taller plants, streak the lawns towards the cliff edge. The Mexican succulent *Furcraea bedinghausii* produces huge candelabras of pendant, lime-green flowers up to five metres high, while *Echium pininana*, from the Canary Islands, stabs the sky with tapering lavender-blue flower spikes up to three-and-a-half metres tall. Says Susan: "Not many property owners in New Zealand are brave enough to install formal gardens any more. They tend to be more expensive because of the structural elements and upkeep needed to keep their lines clean and sharp. Also, the trend today is to use native New Zealand plants in naturalistic ways. But a sunny cliff-top space like this, with mountains to the west and ocean to the east, seemed to need a controlling hand to establish some orderliness with geometric shapes and long vistas, and we think the formal design succeeds beautifully."

FAR LEFT, TOP: *Lime green flower stems of Mexican* Furcraea bedinghausii *reach five metres high.*
FAR LEFT, BOTTOM: *Coast road below Winterhome, with Marlborough rock daisies* (Pachystegia insignis) *growing wild along the cliffs.*
LEFT: *Dramatic lavender-blue spires of* Echium pininana.

Cliff-Top

Kaikoura Garden with a Holy Chiwallies View

Nowhere in all New Zealand do the Pacific Ocean and the coastline meet in more spectacular fashion than beside the historic whaling settlement of Kaikoura, now famous for whale-watching and tasty crayfish. The rugged Kaikoura Peninsula juts out into the ocean, creating a pair of sweeping horseshoe beaches and providing cliff-top views that encompass a spectacular coastal panorama.

A short distance offshore, a deep ocean trench is a rich source of food for all kinds of marine life, including migrating sperm whales as they head to or from Cook Strait, while inland, within full view of the home of Robert and Martha Wagoner, across a glittering blue bay, rise the awesome Kaikoura Ranges, snow-capped for much of the year.

ABOVE: *Native pink manuka in flower with yellow buttonbush* (Cephalanthus *spp.*).
RIGHT: *View from deck of the main house, with New Zealand 'Dazzler' flax in a planter, French lavender beside the deck and mature macrocarpa overlooking Kaikoura Bay below snow-covered Kaikoura Ranges.*

Robert is a potter and mixed-media artist, and it was on a visit to a fellow potter ten years ago that he was drawn to the cliff-top where he and Martha now have their home. On a weekend away from Christchurch, their third South Island place of residence since emigrating from America in 1971, they inspected the property, and when Robert saw the view he exclaimed "Holy chiwallies!" The place then was raw land, a windswept meadow with a lone tree – a dense macrocarpa – which some local residents expected the Wagoners to cut down to improve the view. Instead, Robert saw the tree as a bonus and pruned it judiciously to make a living sculpture, with the view to be enjoyed through its spreading limbs. Recalls Martha: "Just buying the land was enough for me at the time. I thought we would put a caravan on the site for a few years. However, Robert's vision, together with financial assistance from my widowed mother, who lived with us in Christchurch, resulted in a much more substantial holiday house. Robert used a kit from *Colonial Homes* magazine for the basic design, adapting it to make two self-contained apartments."

After raising two boys, Seth and Luke, and the death of Martha's mother, the Wagoners followed the suggestion of two Kaikoura artists of moving to the cliff-top and setting up a gallery with them. Martha now runs the gallery, on Kaikoura's main street, and it serves as an outlet for Robert's artistic endeavours. Some of his works are also incorporated into the cliff-top garden, from gateway stones resembling moa eggs, to large black pots with a shiny finish and whimsical pieces in Dr Seuss shapes and colours.

Robert built a studio on the highest part of the property, and, as the spirit moved him, began landscaping a garden not only to provide an inspirational view from the studio window, but also to serve as an attractive surrounding to the house. Because the site is exposed to burning sun and dessicating winds, plant selections are limited. In addition to some New Zealand natives, such as manuka, flax and tussocks, the greatest successes are African proteas, daisies and poker plants.

A curving driveway leads onto the exposed property, crossing a natural-looking stream that cuts diagonally through the garden to the cliff-top. The edges of the stream are planted with an assortment of drought-tolerant perennials, flowering shrubs and ornamental grasses. A low bank and the house hide the magnificent panorama beyond the cliff-top. This is revealed suddenly either on entering the living room, with its large picture window overlooking the bay and mountains, or on crossing a wooden deck wrapped around the front of the house.

Raised planters at the entrance to the house contain mostly salad crops, while the spidery orange flowers of South African leucospermums contrast spectacularly with the blue of the ocean. In an adjacent grassy meadow – a nature reserve protected from development – skylarks climb high into the sky, singing melodiously. When the creative juices dry up, all Robert requires to get them flowing again is to sit in the swing-seat that hangs from a low branch of the old macrocarpa and take in the "holy chiwallies" view.

Top, left to right: *South African pincushion protea* (Leucospermum cordifolium) *thrives among coastal breezes; examples of Robert's pottery; French lavender blooms earlier than the English; Moss-like pearlwort* (Sagina subulata) *creeps between stepping stones; African daisies bloom in the shelter of a macrocarpa trunk; Swing bench attached to macrocarpa limb.*
Left: *Stream with mostly native plants, including New Zealand flax, tussock grasses and manuka.*

Robyn's Cottage

An Artist's Great Little City Garden

obyn Kilty is a multifaceted Christchurch garden designer who studied painting at Ilam School of Fine Art, University of Canterbury. When she is not at her drawing board or making changes to clients' gardens, she is usually in her cottage garden making further embellishments to its daring design, or painting and drawing in her studio.

Recent travels to California, France, England, Scotland and Wales focused on visiting gardens in search of fresh inspiration, and art galleries to satisfy a passion for modern art. Active in the local community, Robyn helped to form the Friends of Beverley Park Heritage Rose Garden. With support from the Englefield residents' association and the parks and gardens department of the Christchurch City Council, she designed the garden as a new-millennium project. It contains 150 specimens of 40 different varieties of rose. Once the garden had been established, Robyn formed a group of helpers to carry out regular maintenance, such as deadheading, pruning, shaping and weeding.

PREVIOUS PAGE TOP LEFT: *Gaudi-inspired water feature.*
PREVIOUS PAGE RIGHT: *White bench with a high arched backrest, painted white to echo the white wisteria blooms.*
TOP: *Slatted gate screens the side garden from a busy Christchurch street.*
ABOVE LEFT: *Garden shed framed by a pair of apricot trees not only provides storage space but also an appealing focal point for the back garden.*
ABOVE RIGHT: *Courtyard off the kitchen furnished for outdoor entertaining.*

During the years of European settlement, notably in the 1860s, the Englefield housing area grew out of two farms – Englefield and Linwood. Tucked between Linwood and Fitzgerald Avenues and Avonside Drive, it included streets of Victorian workers' cottages, some of which are still reasonably preserved and part of the focus of a local initiative to designate the area a historic district. Robyn's cottage is one of these, probably built around 1870.

Although Robyn's garden is colourful through all seasons, the *Press* has described her tiny front garden at Christmas as "a seasonal joy" on account of an exquisite green-and-red colour combination that contrasts vividly with the cottage's blue weatherboards and corrugated-iron roof. Most conspicuous are the flush of scarlet from a climbing rose – 'Parkdirektor Riggers' – trained over an entrance gate archway, the chocolate-red blooms of a bushy 'Colourbreak' hybrid tea rose, and the orange-red flowers of *Rosa moyesii* 'Geranium', which arches its prickly canes high in the sky and becomes covered in scarlet hips in late summer and autumn. On opposite sides of the front steps, low bushy mounds of scarlet 'Eyeopener' miniature roses ensure that one's entire field of vision is filled with shades of red and green against a sheet of blue. Accompanying the parade of red rose blossoms are red-flowering perennials, including cinnamon-red *Achillea*, blood-red *Abutilon*, red spires of *Lobelia cardinalis*, and scarlet nasturtiums that thread their succulent leaves and stems through a low wooden fence between red brick pillars. Echoing the red flowers is a scarlet-painted door set with stained-glass windows, while fragrant potted topiary rosemary sentinels soften the expanse of blue weatherboarding.

"My first love is painting," Robyn explains. "But the building of patterns and structures in my garden, enhanced by planting, has become my art as well. The idea of using mosaic and the organic form of a water feature along the narrow side garden was inspired by Gaudi and his wonderful mosaics, primarily at Guell Parc in Barcelona. However, the forms and patterns I finally made became less and less Gaudi and more and more me. The way that structures are enhanced by plants is all part of my vision."

From the entrance to the side garden through a high slatted gate, a brick-and-mosaic path leads the eye through a white wisteria-clad arbour, past the water feature to a large white slatted bench with a bowed backrest, made to Robyn's own design. Running the length of the fence and angling around the bench is a shrubbery featuring mostly native plants, including a handsome mountain cabbage tree (*Cordyline indivisa*), several wheki tree ferns (*Dicksonia squarrosa*), colonies of ground ferns, and several colourful hybrid flaxes. Behind the oversize bench are two silvery-leaved plants –

Astelia chathamica 'Silver Spear' and *Olearia cheesmanii*, a variety of native tree daisy.

Turning the corner, the path leads between a pair of apricot trees, their trunks trimmed of lower branches so their outlines frame a garden shed, which marks the limit of the backyard. Along the path, wands of foxgloves strike through low edgings of silvery lavender cotton.

"I'm happy to see New Zealand gardeners becoming more original, cutting their ties to old England," declares Robyn. "We're learning to use materials of our own, like riverstones, driftwood, and garden structures made from twisted manuka branches and other distinctive native timbers. No longer is it necessary to have a Lutyens bench to be considered a sophisticated gardener when we have the capacity to create our own designs. And why have beech or boxwood hedging when New Zealand hebe, coprosma and totara hedges are just as functional and more original?"

However, Robyn insists she is not a native-plant purist. "I find that a bit of a strait-jacket. I prefer to be eclectic. I love the challenge of putting different and unlikely things together."

Robyn's advice to anyone designing a garden for a confined space is not to plant too much of anything or clutter a compact area with too many structural features. "One bold feature in a confined space is usually enough. A large chunky table and chairs in a small courtyard probably shouldn't have an ostentatious fountain as well. In my courtyard I use groups of low potted plants at the edges of the sitting area for decorative effect. If shade is desired, I recommend just one or two trees, perhaps a lacy-foliaged golden gleditsia. In the sitting area of my courtyard there is no space for a garden, so I use four matching blue pots – one in each corner – containing limes. The wisteria overhead produces much-needed summer shade, but lets the sun through when the leaves drop during winter. Colour can be bright, but not chaotic, with lots of surrounding green. Opposites on the colour wheel are always a good guide – red and green, blue and orange, yellow and purple. There should be a flow to a garden, more of a few species rather than less of a lot. "

Robyn also believes a garden should reflect the needs of its owners. "My garden has become an outdoor studio for me where I am endlessly creating a comforting environment – sometimes quirky, sometimes romantic. But I also need a garden to be a serene place which harmonises and feeds the soul," she concludes.

TOP: *Cottage from the street in early summer displays a predominantly red-and-green colour harmony, with climbing roses over an entrance arbour, 'Empress of India' nasturtiums, red daylilies and cinnamon-red yarrow.*
ABOVE LEFT: *Climbing rose 'Crepuscule' creates a complementary colour contrast with the indigo blue trim of the window.*
ABOVE RIGHT: *'Colourbreak' red roses echo the colour of the front door.*

Gethsemane

Biblical Garden with an Ocean View

The coastal community of Sumner is just a few minutes' drive from the bustling heart of Christchurch, and a favourite place for day-trippers and holiday-makers to walk the beach, enjoy refreshment at a café, picnic by the sea and swim beneath cliff palisades. With houses crowding the steep hillsides, it seems an unlikely place for a large and diverse garden, yet perched on the highest point of Revelation Drive is just such a place. Gethsemane enjoys breathtaking views beyond Sumner Beach, across the glittering waters of Pegasus Bay to the majestic Kaikoura Ranges in the distance, their peaks often dusted with snow.

ABOVE: *'Wedding Day' climbing rose shelters a garden bench.*
RIGHT: *View overlooking Gethsemane towards Pegasus Bay with masses of marguerite daisies in the foreground.*

132

Established in 1987 by Bev and Ken Loader as a romantic garden and a tribute to the teachings of Christianity, Gethsemane contains a small chapel where couples can be married surrounded by a series of garden "rooms", formed out of a series of trellises and walls that spell the name Gethsemane, each room or letter designed as a self-contained theme garden. Separated from these flower gardens by a car park is a potager garden, where vegetables and herbs grow in raised beds arranged in a labyrinth design. Grape vines and espaliered fruit trees, including lemons, are trained up strong trellises, and these fruit abundantly among beets, cabbages, carrots and other common food crops.

Gethsemane is rich not only in unusual plants, especially flowering vines and perennials, but also in decorative structures. The chapel is made of trelliswork, and most of the garden rooms are entered through a rose-covered archway. A herb-knot garden within the floral area is designed around a Star of David clipped from green lavender cotton, while further up the slope is a Star of Bethlehem, and beyond that a grove of olive trees.

An all-white garden is separated by a gravel path from a naturalistic water garden, where the fronds of native tree ferns and the rhubarb-like leaves of gunneras shelter water lilies from the wind. Several viewing platforms peek above the burgeoning vegetation to take in breathtaking views of the wider garden and the Pacific Ocean beyond.

The Loaders are avid plant collectors, and though they used to offer potted versions of almost everything in the garden, Gethsemane is now strictly a display garden. South African gazanias and marguerite daisies are a special feature, forming generous drifts along a dry, sunny bank at the top of the garden. Penstemons and heucheras add sparkle to a spacious perennial garden crammed with varieties only recently introduced into commerce, many from obscure British and north-west-Pacific breeders.

Of especial interest to children is a collection of miniature buildings representing biblical cities, and another of miniature animals depicting the story of Noah's ark. A formal rose garden is laid out as a maze, and a series of ten rose-covered archways forms a bridal path, leading to the chapel. Strategically placed along paths are container plantings – not only annuals, such as Flanders Field poppies, but also edible plants, such as silver beet, and alpines in tufa troughs.

Bev has a warning for me: "We are not an easy garden to photograph. The sunlight up here is bright, and it tends to produce a harsh contrast of sunlight and shadow that film cannot record as effectively as the human eye, but photographers love the place and keep returning to catch it in all weathers and all seasons."

OPPOSITE: *Chapel made from trelliswork is popular for wedding ceremonies. Parterre hedges in the foreground are clipped from grey lavender cotton (*Santolina chamaecyparissus*).*
TOP: *Perennial garden in summer, with a drift of red carnations making a bold splash of colour.*
BOTTOM: *Calamondin orange makes a decorative accent in the vegetable garden.*

She explains that the garden's exposure to sun and wind has dictated a heavy emphasis on drought-tolerant plants, such as agapanthus, red-hot pokers, regal geraniums and red valerian. Casting an eye at the cloudless blue sky, she sighs with obvious hope for rainfall. "For me the most enchanting time for the garden is after a storm when the sky is still overcast, and the colours of leaves and flowers are intensified by the diffused light and refreshing rain. I wish everyone could see it then."

For frequent visitors to the garden, the speed of change seems phenomenal. An example of the spontaneity with which things happen is the wedding chapel. During a break from his labours, a young garden worker remarked that he was planning to get married and would like nothing better than to tie the knot on the spot on which he was standing. The fact that the date fixed for the wedding was only five weeks away did not deter the Loaders, and the chapel was completed in time.

Fertile soil and frequent deadheading are vital to the maintenance of the bold floral displays. The indigenous soil is heavy clay, but when it is mixed with stable manure and seaweed compost it provides excellent anchorage for plants so exposed to wind.

Although the biblical theme and spiritual messages of Gethsemane are an unusual focus for a garden, they are understated. Such is the design integrity of the gardens' rooms, and so dominant the rich plant palette, the religious elements are not obvious. It is a garden that anyone, no matter what their faith or beliefs, can admire and find uplifting.

OPPOSITE: *White marguerite daisies and 'Wedding Day' climbing roses combine with the silvery lavender cotton to create an all-white garden theme.*
INSET: *Chives partnered with cabbage in the herb garden where edible plants are grown in raised beds.*
ABOVE LEFT: *Peruvian lily (*Alstromeria *hybrid, 'Little Eleanor') lights up the perennial garden.*
ABOVE RIGHT: *Small pond with leaves of giant gunnera dominating the plantings.*

137

Ohinetahi

Architectural Integrity

When early immigrants to the South Island entered the port of Lyttelton, after more than a hundred days at sea on the voyage from England, they were eager to begin life in a land described to them as paradise. But that impression depended on whether the sheltered harbour was bathed in sunlight or darkened by thick cloud cover. On a fine day, the aquamarine water and purple-hued hills looked inviting. But if the sky was overcast and there was a blustery wind carrying rain, the amphitheatre of hills had a forbidding air. Many immigrants felt such a depth of disappointment as they approached the wharf that they refused to leave ship, and took passage home without even stepping ashore. Which is a pity, because just over the brow of the coastal hills the beautiful Canterbury Plain, with deep alluvial soil and a Mediterranean climate, stretched to the foothills of the snow-capped Southern Alps.

ABOVE: *Suspension bridge across the ravine.*
RIGHT: *The rose garden at Ohinetahi features boxwood topiary and mostly hybrid tea roses for cutting.*

At the top of Lyttelton Harbour, near Governors Bay, is one of New Zealand's most celebrated gardens: Ohinetahi. The name has various meanings, including "only one daughter".

The owner, architect Sir Miles Warren, designed the garden around an 1850s stone house with his sister, Pauline Trengrove (a painter), and her architect husband, John. The result is that it features not only a number of structural accents, but also a choice collection of plants, particularly roses and trees. There are a lot of brick paths, stone walls and clipped boxwood hedges that define self-contained garden "rooms", but the backdrop of rugged hills and glittering bay help temper the surfeit of formality. "I like to think of the garden as a formal framework with a luxuriant profusion of plants" is how Sir Miles summarises their collaboration.

Over a period of 19 years, the three collaborators transformed neglected remnants of a former garden into a spectacular fusion of horticultural and architectural integrity. All three used to live at Ohinetahi, but eventually the Trengroves left to build their own home, with a new four-hectare formal garden, near Christchurch.

Today, Sir Miles delights in allowing visitors into his garden and explaining its design. "An architectural structure is mostly bricks and mortar, and once you have the durable elements in place they stay that way. But with gardens, each plant is constantly changing, and so much more forethought is needed because small trees can become large and out of scale, and plants like perennials can be aggressive and soon exceed their bounds. Also, unless a garden is cared for continuously, it can quickly revert to wilderness."

He believes the key to Ohinetahi's appeal is its "strong bones", especially the evergreen hedges that define many of the self-contained spaces. He concedes that the large expanses of walls may need mellowing with vines, and that boxwood must be trimmed three times a year to keep its lines clean and sharp. "But hedges, fences, paths and walls all help to outline a basic floor plan, into which more colourful plants like roses and perennials can be planted for softening and seasonal effects."

At the heart of the garden's formal arrangement is a series of long, straight dissecting axes. One leads from the house across a rectangle of lawn and along a brick path to a traditional gazebo that echoes the white arches of the veranda. A cross axis starts at the top of a steep hill, with views of the bay, and descends in a series of terraces.

A rose garden on the bay side of the veranda features a parterre of ten boxwood squares punctuated with spirals of topiary, each square containing a single variety of hybrid tea rose. When the roses are in full flower, the topiary forms are barely visible. But in winter, when the roses are pruned, the topiary is more prominent and adds to the garden's charm.

However, the garden is not all straight lines and circles. Running between the house and the west boundary is a steep ravine that has been converted into a bush garden. Sir Miles explains: "The contrast between the two areas – one bright and formal and the other shady and informal – is unexpected. A sleek suspension bridge spans the ravine as a continuation of the cross axis from the formal garden. Visitors step off the bridge and are immediately confronted with a series of shaded paths leading down to a natural stream edged with moisture-loving plants like primulas, hostas and rhododendrons."

The first house built on the property was a small seaside cottage. Then, in the 1860s, an eminent botanist and ornithologist, T. H. Potts, became owner, and he replaced the cottage with a more substantial three-storey structure, made of locally quarried sandstone block, with a veranda all the way round. "A succession of owners followed, the structure suffered, the roof leaked badly, and there was a lot to do when we bought it in 1977," Sir Miles remembers. "When I first moved here the house was incidental. We were more attracted by the coastal setting and the mountainous backdrop, and its potential to be a beautiful garden."

His most recent additions include a stone tower from which to view the house and garden, and an art gallery set below and beside the rose garden, facing the bay.

What is most surprising about the grounds is that they are contained within a hectare-and-a-quarter. It seems larger because not only can visitors see well beyond the boundaries of the garden to distant hillsides and glimmering tidal water, but the paths are designed to go up and down slopes, and to backtrack. Also, the hedges and walls ensure you never see the entire garden from any one viewpoint.

In 1774 it was Humphrey Repton who used the term "landscape gardening" to describe what he did for English estates, but it was the late Frederick Law Homestead, designer of New York's Central Park, who coined the term "landscape architect" to describe himself. At the time it was a controversial choice of words, for it seemed a contradiction in terms, architecture, as applied to buildings, often introducing ugliness into a landscape. But Ohinetahi shows clearly how architecture in the form of imaginative garden structures and well-chosen plants can enhance a beautiful natural environment.

LEFT: *Overall view of main homestead showing part of Governor's Bay. Celtic stone plinth and Grecian columns provide diverse architectural accents.*

Tree Crop Farm

Garden Whimsy and Bush Baths in Akaroa

Grehan Valley Road is a steep uphill climb from the main road between Christchurch and the Akaroa wharf. Lifestyle blocks are set well back and generally veiled by trees. The valley is sheltered and cloaked in native bush, and the dawn chorus so melodious an overnight guest at Tree Crop Farm thought it was piped music. Where the road ends, a public footpath runs past the farm – named after an orchard of nut trees planted by early French immigrants – to connect with a network of scenic walking tracks, including an exhilarating three-hour tramp to uninhabited parts of the coast.

ABOVE: *View of the garden from the veranda with an easy chair covered in sheepskin and a table set for breakfast.*
RIGHT: *View downstream over clumps of French lavender, lupins and bronze-leaf fennel to the historic homestead.*

Bordered by rough fieldstone walls, the gravel drive leading to the homestead curves past an organic vegetable garden with local manuka sticks formed into "tepees" for vines to climb. Opposite is a one-storey indigo-painted house with a blue corrugated-iron roof, smoke curling into the sky from a crackling log fire. A part-sod 1850s colonial cottage, the house seems Spartan at first glance, but at the rear is a spacious veranda with views across a sparkling stream to a line of grassy hills that shelter the farm from northerly winds off the Pacific Ocean. A group of comfortable lounging chairs draped with fleecy sheepskins – produced on the property – faces a sheep pasture and the foot-worn track that trampers follow to the coastal footpath beyond the brow of a hill.

Passers-by and visitors to the homestead are invited to pause, take a seat on the veranda and enjoy refreshment. Delicious boysenberry and blackberry fruit juices, herbal teas and home-made date bread are not the only inducements to stop and rest. There is also a well-stocked library of travel magazines and paperback books.

FAR LEFT, TOP TO BOTTOM: *Mexican-style chiminee decorates the edge of a meadow garden; Window of a guest cottage garlanded with clematis; Wild meadow filled with artichokes as they would grow along clifftop meadows of their native Greece; Bottle collection at the entrance to the meadow garden.*
LEFT: *View from the top of the property through spires of giant echium over the roof of the homestead.*
ABOVE: *Guest shares her breakfast with newly hatched ducklings.*

This is the domain of owner Lynne Alexander, semi-retired from a career in journalism and broadcasting, who, apart from her love of gardening, likes nothing more than to make people laugh. Hanging from the rafters of the veranda by the hundred, and scattered about the garden, are tablets of driftwood and smooth beach stones inscribed with a fascinating collection of anecdotes and witticisms. Visitors are encouraged to contribute their own for Lynne's approval. On a stone seat overhung with liquorice-scented lovage, a wooden board declares: "Outside a dog a book is a man's best friend. Inside a dog is too dark to read," attributed to Groucho Marx. A peaked wooden mailbox states: "One good turn gets all the blankets." One of Lynne's favourites is: "If things get any worse, I'll have to ask you to stop helping me," recalling as it does the years of struggle to establish her dream home.

Tree Crop Farm occupies 26 hectares of native bush, sheep pasture and coastal meadows. The homestead was dilapidated when Lynne purchased it in the late 1980s, having returned from Europe with a toddler she wanted to raise in the country. Juggling several jobs to pay for improvements, she has become largely self-sufficient, raising her own food and renting out three rustic huts, each in its own wild-garden setting complete with bush bath – a cast-iron bathtub set over a pit so it can be heated from beneath by a log fire.

Lynne's garden philosophy is to maintain a casual, wild appearance with as little effort as possible. Except for her large organic vegetable garden – all raised beds – she doesn't have time to take care of formal garden spaces, so she allows the grass to grow tall. She cuts paths through it with a weed-eater, scattering seed among islands of bare soil to create naturalistic wild-flower colonies.

A lot of garden chores are done by WWOOFers – Willing Workers on Organic Farms – mostly young European backpackers who trade garden and farm work for room and board. Some have been skilled carpenters and stonemasons, and have helped to make the rustic gates, twig furniture and stone walls that decorate the property. Lynne encourages them to stay a while, switching them to different parts of the property to avoid tedium – perhaps clearing her meadow of thistles one day, making compost another, even keeping the creek clear of debris. For those working along the banks of the creek there is an iron bedstead in midstream, shaded by an old overhanging walnut tree – a good place to take a rest and doze to the music of rippling water. Downstream, slung above the water, is a hammock, available to guests in the lower hut.

Herbs, tucked into every nook and cranny, grow in all parts of the garden. As Lynne explains: "Most herbs are carefree and don't demand fertile soil. I not only grow them for culinary use, I also enjoy their spicy fragrances. I love to tie bunches of herbs together for kindling – like bay, lavender and eucalyptus – because burning the fragrant faggots releases their wonderful aromas, and the coastal breeze wafts the smoke into all corners of the property."

Lemon balm and anise hyssop are favourite flavourings for herbal teas, hot and iced. "Lemon balm steeped in ice-cold water makes a wonderful refreshing drink," Lynne enthuses. "Even fennel with water is lovely." She always has bottles of both available for visitors and WWOOFers.

But of all the plants that thrive at Tree Crop Farm, the artichoke is queen. With its large, silvery, sharply indented leaves and bristly flower head, edible in bud, this giant thistle-like plant is grown for food in the vegetable garden, as an ornamental along the side of the house, and naturalised with wild lavender, foxgloves and poppies on a slope facing the veranda, its bold purple flowers black with bumblebees, creating a scene more reminiscent of Provence than New Zealand. "When its woody stems turn brown and brittle in winter, I cut them for kindling, and renewed growth comes up from the roots," explains Lynne. "I could never be without artichokes."

The only spoilers in the landscape are possums, which live in the bush and encroach into the garden at night, searching for tender shoots and fat rosebuds. They will strip a climbing rose clean over several forays, though persistent trapping helps to control them. Overnight guests, wrapped in warm possum-skin blankets for morning breakfast on the veranda, delight in the colourful, carefree atmosphere and the prospect of a family of fearless ducklings venturing up from the stream to share breakfast leftovers.

LEFT: *Rustic bench with example of humorous quotations that adorn the veranda and garden.*
ABOVE: *White lupins and arum lilies create an all-white theme.*

147

Grehan Lea

Barbara Lea Taylor's Cottage Garden

When *New Zealand Gardener* magazine recently conducted a poll among its members, Barbara Lea Taylor won the vote for most popular garden writer, and now there is scarcely an issue in which she does not appear. An expert on heritage roses, she lectures widely throughout New Zealand, presenting the pros and cons of the varieties she likes, and tactfully fielding questions from the audience about the merits of varieties she doesn't admire.

Barbara gardens along a stream that tumbles down Grehan Valley to the harbour-side township of Akaroa, on Banks Peninsula, and lives in a cottage that could be straight from the pages of a Beatrix Potter children's book, complete with romantic rustic arbours covered in scented rambling roses, and sweeps of lavender. Mauve poppies and pink granny's bonnets self-sow generously into every scrap of bare soil, their petals shimmering and sparkling among the rose bushes.

ABOVE: *Barbara's cottage and French lavender.*
RIGHT: *View across the cottage garden filled with roses and lavender to a sunny hillside where mostly native trees and shrubs present a tapestry of foliage contrasts.*

Barbara was drawn to the property in the late 1980s when she was living in Christchurch, attracted as she was by Akaroa's slower pace of life and the peacefulness of its rural setting. The cottage was ensconced on the side of a hill, screened from the road by trees, the sheltered blue harbour just a short walk away, and offering views from the living room of green hills covered in sheep pasture and remnants of native bush. A stand of ancient kahikatea trees on a far slope she estimates to be 700 years old. They give the valley a prehistoric appearance – "Also an excuse for me to have a scruffy garden," Barbara adds.

When she moved there, Akaroa was a quiet backwater, a tedious two-hour drive from Christchurch along a tortuous road, and so provided exactly the seclusion she cherished. Though tourists have since discovered the charms of the little township, and a parade of gourmet restaurants, wineries, motels and souvenir shops now peppers the main road, Akaroa retains much of its sleepy enchantment, and Grehan Lea – Barbara's picture-postcard cottage – is the perfect place for a prolific writer to work undisturbed.

One of the oldest residences on Banks Peninsula, dating back to 1852, when the first British settlers arrived, it was built to house the manager of a flour mill. A party of French immigrants had arrived earlier, in 1840, and established vineyards and orchards. They also brought with them rooted cuttings of roses that reminded them of home.

When Barbara saw her future home it was in poor condition, having been used for many years mostly as a holiday cottage, and it needed a lot of alterations to make it comfortable. The cold winters and warm summers of Banks Peninsula were ideal for growing a rose garden, and there was plenty of animal manure available locally to keep the greedy roots well fed.

Previously a teacher of fourth-form teenagers, in Melbourne, Barbara yearned for a more relaxed lifestyle and wanted to write for a living. She chose gardening as a specialist subject, as well as travel, having discovered a demand for "gardeners who wrote, not writers who gardened". She began writing for the *Christchurch Star* and *New Zealand Gardener*, and benefited from the nation-wide gardening boom of the early 1980s. She became hooked on roses after reading the late rosarian Nancy Steen's book *The Charm of Old Roses* as long ago as 1960. She also acknowledges the influence of Trevor

Christchurch, and the Bolton Street Cemetery, Wellington, because it is "small, uncontrived and informal".

Barbara's favourite roses are all rugosas. "They are tough as old boots, disease-free, maintenance-free, and most have a fruity fragrance." She especially recommends 'Hansa', not only for its large double wine-purple flowers, but also for its heavy fragrance. "The perfume is almost as strong as 'Reine des Violettes', a double purple-mauve hybrid perpetual introduced in 1860. One bloom of either can fill an entire room with fragrance."

Barbara's favourite modern rose-breeder is British rosarian David Austin. "He began crossing old garden roses onto modern hybrids and discarded anything among the progeny that didn't look old-fashioned – quite the opposite of what other rose breeders were doing. He then selected for repeat bloom and good fragrance."

Austin's roses, sold under the brand name English Roses, frequently have names chosen for their historical significance or Shakespearean associations. "One of the most free-flowering in my garden is 'Belle Story', named for the first nursing sister in World War II. A soft, semi-double, introduced in 1984, it is a wonderful shrub rose for my garden."

Barbara acknowledges that modern hybrid teas (bred for large blooms) and floribundas (bred for multiple blooms on a truss) are still popular, but she regards the majority rather soulless compared with the cupped, swirling petal formations and button centres of most heritage roses.

Red honeysuckle, blue wisteria, pink clematis and white jasmine mingle in her garden with climbing roses. A gate with a criss-cross pattern of wild manuka branches opens onto a footbridge that leads over the stream into a sunny meadow and a small vineyard where 40 Chardonnay vines produce bountiful harvests. Rather than try to keep the sloping meadow mown, Barbara cuts paths through it with a mower and allows annuals to seed in the long grass.

When it's time to meet a writing deadline, Barbara retreats to her veranda, where she sits at a table with her notepad and a cup of tea. Beyond the veranda the stream gurgles, cabbage trees rustle their lance-like leaves, foxgloves sway, songbirds sing and sweet fragrances pervade the vibrating atmosphere, while at the table the creative juices start to flow.

Griffith, "the patriarch of roses in New Zealand". She has since served nine years as editor of the Heritage Rose Society magazine.

Barbara considers Parnell Rose Garden, in Auckland, in particular its Nancy Steen Garden, as one of the country's best because it displays not only a big selection of modern roses, but also, in a separate section, a fine collection of old garden roses and species roses. Also high on her list of must-see New Zealand rose gardens are the Jessie Calder Rose Garden, in Queen's Park, Invercargill, the Hagley Park rose garden,

FAR LEFT, TOP: *Annual poppies flaunt satin-like petals and plump seed pods in the cottage garden.*
ABOVE LEFT: *Cottage from the hillside meadow showing David Austin rose 'Belle Story' spilling into the path. A gate made from manuka branches adds just the right touch of rustic charm to the rose-covered cottage almost hidden by burgeoning greenery.*

Trott's Garden

A Fondness for Foliage

*V*ita Sackville-West, founder of Britain's famous Sissinghurst Castle Garden, declared that her design philosophy was to have the strictest formality in layout and the utmost informality in plantings. As a result the view from her castle tower was of a decorative grid of garden compartments – and, beyond, the bucolic beauty of the Weald of Kent.

Rather than a castle tower, Alan and Catherine Trott's two-and-three-quarter-hectare garden near Ashburton has a belvedere at its centre, mounted on stilts so that, on one side, it has a bird's-eye view of compartments defined by closely clipped macrocarpa hedges, like the hemlock hedges of Sissinghurst. On the other three sides it looks across free-flowing lawns outlined with perennial borders, shrubberies, and a spring-fed creek that flows through a bog garden before meandering out of the tree-sheltered property.

ABOVE: *Himalayan white birch.*
RIGHT: *The bog garden in summer, with vigorous clumps of gunnera, hostas and astilbes planted beside a boardwalk. Insets, top to bottom: Penstemon hybrid 'Drinkwater'; Japanese coral bark maple; Scotch thistle and poker plants.*

Says Alan: "The most challenging site on which to make a good garden is flat ground like we have on the Canterbury Plains, because hilly terrain can be landscaped in tiers or terraces to present a dramatic setting that fills your entire field of vision with interest. The trick to making a flat site interesting is to ensure there are lots of corners to negotiate, and to have breathtaking views around every corner."

To achieve this sense of discovery, the Trotts rely heavily on trees and evergreen rhododendrons, which they use to create screens beside paths. Rhododendrons are so prolific that when one outgrows its bounds or doesn't seem to be pulling its weight by blooming well enough, Alan digs it up and replaces it with a different tree or shrub species, usually one with colourful wintry bark, such as yellow-stemmed dogwood, cherries with coppery bark or white birch. "We don't want to be known only as a rhododendron garden," he insists. "We want people to realise this is a garden for all seasons, with perennials, bog plants and rare trees."

With help from their sons – Paul, Hamish and Matthew – the Trotts have developed a garden of such distinction and beauty they have been honoured with the Canterbury Horticultural Society's Award of Excellence. It is difficult to believe such a spacious garden does not have an army of groundsmen.

To help establish the basic structure, or bones, of the garden, the Trotts enlisted the services of Christchurch architect John Trengrove, who designed the formal area to cover a third of the site. The perennial border is unique – 110 metres long, double-sided and filled with strictly herbaceous plants displayed in alcoves. Each alcove has its own theme, such as a fragrance or a specific colour. A separate formal rose garden features 16 beds with 16 roses apiece.

To the south of the macrocarpa hedges, just beyond the formal area, a chapel provides a decorative structural element. Featuring white stucco walls, exposed dark timbers, Gothic windows and a slate roof, it was built in 1916 but eventually ceased to serve as a place of worship and was offered for sale. Alan bought it and moved it to the property, retaining its polished rimu interior, pulpit and altar, and its long narrow pews and dining room with kitchen attached. Now it serves as a place to hold weddings and as a gathering spot where

TOP RIGHT: *Rusty-red blooms of* Euphorbia griffithii *light up the stream.*
RIGHT: *Belvedere provides a high elevation view over the garden.*
OPPOSITE: *White Himalayan birch are a special feature of Trott's Gardens, planted across lawns where lawn shadows become an integral part of the garden design.*

busloads of visitors can hear Alan explain the garden's brief history and design philosophy, which includes the use of foliage to weave a tapestry of greens.

"While some people enjoy instant colour from annuals, in a big garden they give the impression of a quick fix. For me personally, I feel more challenged by seeking visual impact from form and texture rather than gaudy colour. That's why we give a heavy emphasis to trees and shrubs. I like trees with multiple trunks so they can be thinned of cross branches to produce sculptural lines – and, with the coral-bark maple *Acer palmatum* 'Sango Kaku', for example, to expose a warm coral-red glow. Of course there's no secret that white birches look good in a wintry landscape, but few people use the faster-growing river birch, *Betula nigra* 'Uru Tawhai', with its exfoliating, honey-coloured bark."

Alan also recommends the double-flowered 'Lanarth' viburnum for its layered branches studded with fan-shaped white flower clusters, and new pink-flowering forms of Korean dogwood (*Cornus kousa*).

Nowhere is the rich tapestry effect more noticeable than around a pond. Rimmed with a wealth of bog plants, many chosen for spectacular leaves, it is the contrast of monstrous gunneras and large velvety rodgersias with paddle-shaped hostas and ivy-leaved peltyphyllums that creates an indelible impression. Flowering plants such as yellow flag irises, frothy white astilbes and carmine bog primulas are scattered between the bold foliage clumps to create a subtle, understated glittering effect. As Alan explains: "The pond is a big hit with visitors, and I'm always looking at it with a critical eye. The large-leaved plants, like gunneras, can quickly exceed their bounds and look grotesque, so I try to tame the bullies by rigorous dividing, and potting up the division for sale in the nursery, where they are quickly snapped up."

Trott's Garden is situated against a spectacular backdrop of mountains that are snow-covered for much of the year, though windbreak hedges along the boundaries obscure the view in spring and summer – which is why Alan urges visitors to return in autumn and winter, the best time of year to appreciate his rare collection of woody plant varieties.

RIGHT: *Wildlife pond overhung with a white Himalayan birch and bordered with a choice collection of hostas, Japanese irises, astilbes and meadowrue.*
OPPOSITE TOP: *Stream garden meanders under a footbridge and across a sunny meadow. Bog primulas, deciduous azaleas, flag irises and hostas are planted along its length.*
OPPOSITE BOTTOM: *View over macrocarpa hedges to the chapel from the belvedere.*

Parkside

The Pride of a Quarryman's Wife

Oamaru's neat-as-a-pin front yards are bounded by white picket fences and limestone balustrades that enclose flower-beds packed with colour. The locals are so proud of their town's historic business centre of fine neo-classical Victorian architecture that every year they celebrate their Victorian heritage, dressing up in period costume and plying the streets on penny-farthings.

Unfortunately, few visitors stop to explore Oamaru's attractions because most are drawn too strongly by the bigger tourist magnet of Dunedin. But the town is worth a stay of at least a night or two, not only to savour the comfort and hospitality of the recently refurbished Bryden Hotel, in the centre of town, but also to visit the spacious botanical gardens, within walking distance of the hotel, and to watch little blue penguins returning at dusk to their nests along the cliffs.

ABOVE: *Plaster cat decorates a bench.*
RIGHT: *Spires of delphiniums tower above the English-style double perennial border.*

FAR LEFT: *View of double perennial border with balustrade and pedestal of Oamaru limestone as a decorative focal point in the background.*
LEFT: *Rose 'Sally Holmes' softens the lines of a gazebo.*
BELOW: *Pergola made from Oamaru limestone is a centerpiece of the main lawn.*

Between the hotel and the penguin colony is the old business district, where the streets are lined with stone edifices of such bygone grandeur that to tread them feels like walking the old financial district of London or Edinburgh, even if the banks, warehouses, shipping companies and insurance firms of old have largely given way to shops, cafés and restaurants. The impetus for this architectural splendour was the belief among early settlers that Oamaru would be the South Island's main port of entry, but when gold was discovered in Central Otago, Dunedin stole Oamaru's thunder, and so the town never reached the size and importance once expected of it.

The source of the stone from which the grand buildings are made is the Parkside Limestone Quarry, west of town. This is also the site of a magnificent garden designed, planted and maintained by the energetic Linda Wilson with the help of her husband, quarry manager Robert.

Parkside is the only quarry in New Zealand that produces limestone for building. Known as Oamaru stone, it is white and easily sawn. It is quarried from a deposit 40 metres thick before being cut into blocks for building purposes or crushed to make powder for agricultural lime, used to sweeten acid soils. Parkside limestone is considered as high-grade as the best English and French limestones. It was formed 35–40 million years ago when hard-shelled marine organisms accumulated in thick deposits on the sea-floor. The deposits hardened into rock, and unlike many other limestone deposits, which are tainted with debris such as volcanic ash, Oamaru stone is free of impurities, making it suitable for garden ornaments such as pillars, paving and balustrades.

The garden Linda has designed is in a sheltered depression below the family homestead. Initially she planned it as a display garden for her nursery business, but eventually the nursery closed, leaving the space strictly a pleasure garden. At its heart is a "bowl" – a velvet-like free-form lawn with a large arbour at one end, the top covered with an avalanche of *Clematis montana* 'Rubens', and at the other end a herb garden entered through an arbour of heritage climbing roses. The bowl, with encircling borders of perennials and flowering shrubs, is impressive enough, but paths lead off into separate garden "rooms", one comprising a double perennial border with a rustic garden seat at one end and a stone pedestal at the other. A gazebo garden with a pool, and a children's garden planted round a sand pit, are other theme areas. As Linda explains: "I began the nursery as an adjunct to the limestone business, but I realised the commercial emphasis was a distraction and a blight on the aesthetic appeal of the garden. When I took away the commercial aspect I made a more beautiful garden, planting for myself and not to create a sale with what was on display."

With the exception of a handsome colony of variegated mountain flax, native plants are few, for Linda's intention all along was to create an English-style cottage garden, and for that reason roses abound. Her favourites include the yellow David Austin rose 'Graham Thomas' and the large, globular, single white 'Sally Holmes', which from a distance looks like a rhododendron in bloom.

Completely covering an arbour with miniature rose blooms are the apricot-pink 'Phyllis Bide' and deep pink 'Jeanne Lajoie'. A tall bamboo fence covered in jasmine is all that separates this fragrant "secret garden" from a road, but one so little travelled this is a tranquil place to sit, and a favourite family reading spot. Low-growing thyme, tucked among the flagstones, produces an uplifting fragrance whenever it is stepped on.

Among Linda's favourite perennials are blue delphiniums, with black petal centres. "The touch of black produces a richer blue," she observes. Other spire-like plants punctuating the mixed perennial borders are purple foxgloves and yellow king's spear (*Asphodeline lutea*). Linda adores the profusion of dainty blooms on the Mexican daisy (*Erigeron karvinskianus*), and laments the species being placed on the list of New Zealand's most invasive plants. Though it self-seeds readily, its low-growing cushionlike habit produces a sparkle she would miss if it were eradicated.

"A big attraction of living on the edge of Central Otago is the distinct changes of season," she adds. "Winters are cold and frosty, with seasonal snow; spring is lovely with the fresh greens of unfurling leaves; summer is usually warm and sunny, allowing apricots and peaches to ripen to perfection; and autumn is a blaze of russet colours. It's the closest I know to living in paradise."

TOP LEFT: *Native cabbage tree in flower and variegated New Zealand flax line the main driveway.*
BOTTOM LEFT: *Secluded herb garden with cherub sculpture and sundial as decorative accents. Climbing roses 'Phyllis Bide' and 'Jeanne Lajoie' decorate the arbour.*
TOP RIGHT: *Maiden statue and perennial border framed by vines covering the pergola.*
BOTTOM RIGHT: *Main lawn vista viewed from the herb garden, showing rose-covered pergola.*

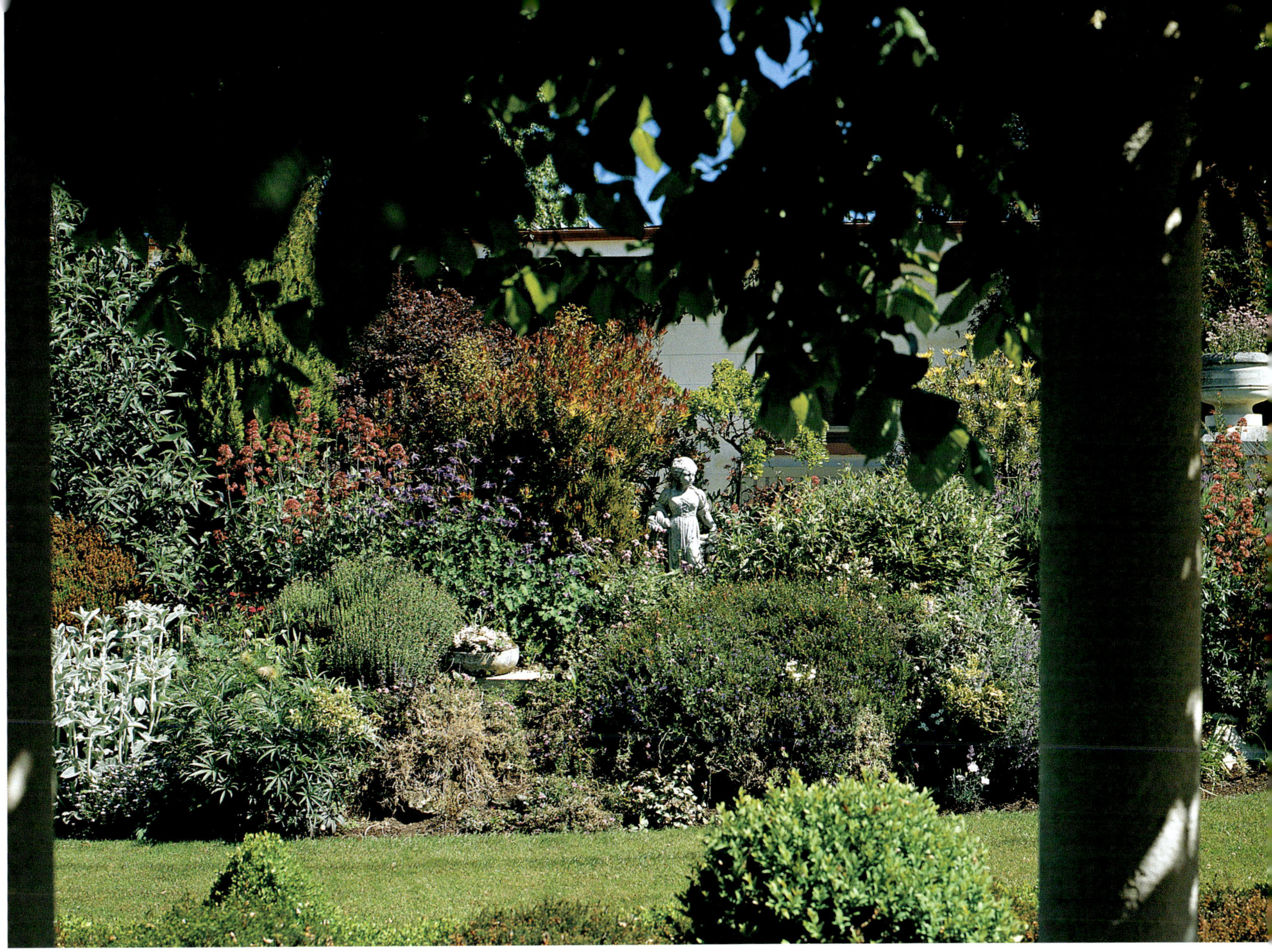

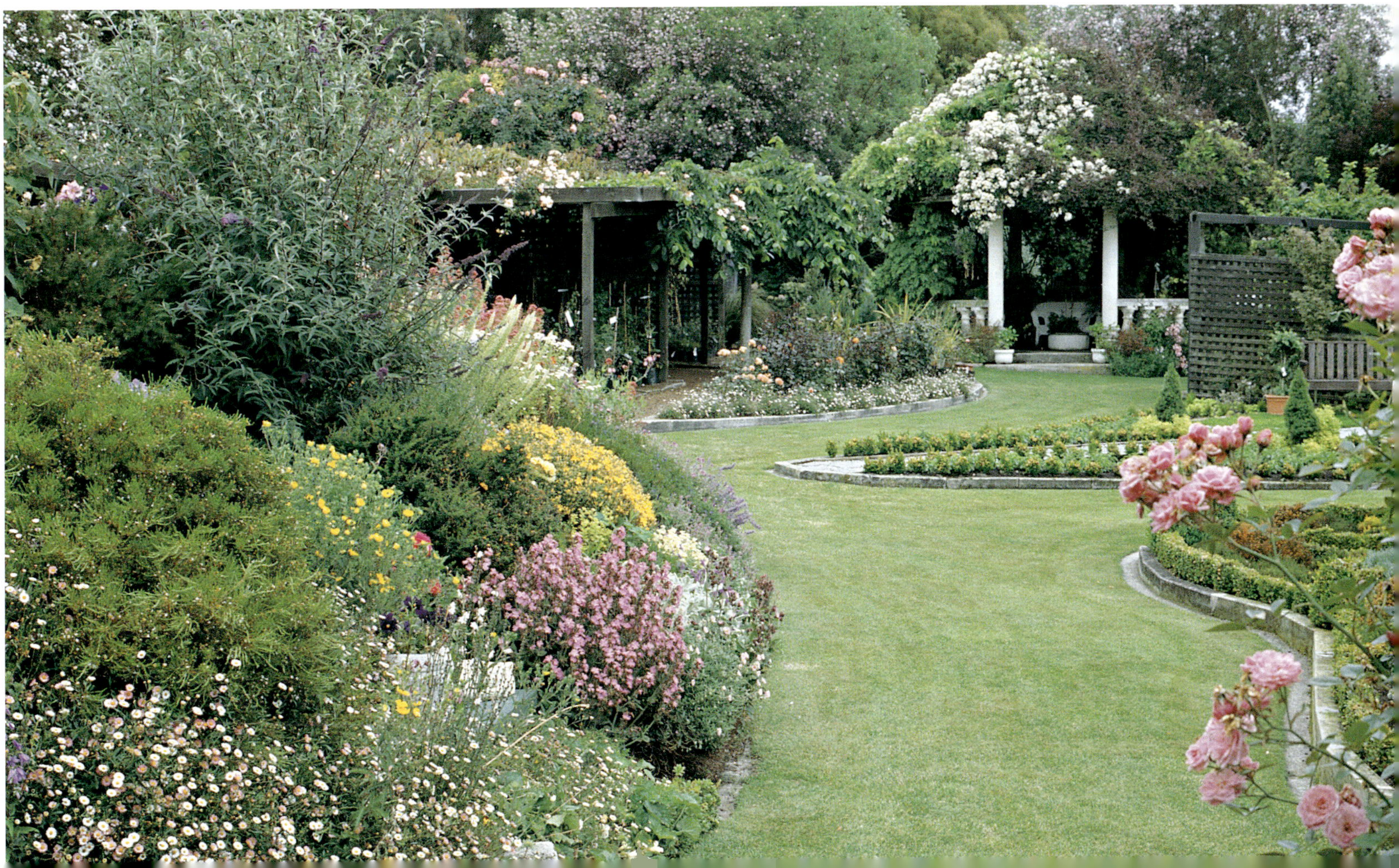

Larnach Castle

Memories of Scotland on the Otago Peninsula

The Battle of Culloden, in 1746, which ended in defeat for the Scottish Highlanders and the Stuart claim to the English throne, took place nearly a hundred years before the European settlement of New Zealand, but the outcome of the battle forced many families to flee Scotland and seek refuge in foreign lands. Many prospered better overseas than they would have done at home, and their success in such colonies as Canada, the USA, Cape Province and Australia prompted other Scots to seek fortunes abroad. Attractions close to a Scotsman's heart abounded in these new worlds – mountains as majestic as the Highlands, and windblown sandy beaches as desolate as the dunes of the Moray Firth and the Western Isles.

ABOVE: *One of a pair of stone lions that stand sentinel at the castle entrance.*
RIGHT: *Larnach Castle with mass planting of fragrant deciduous azaleas above mounds of English lavender that will bloom later in the season. The castle combines elements of Scottish castles in the crenellated walls and towers, and also Australian Victoriana architecture in the gingerbread two-tiered veranda. Located on the narrow Otago Peninsula, the castle commands sea views in three directions.*

The parents of William Larnach were Scottish settlers in Australia. His father had arrived there in 1823 at the age of 19, and William worked for four months as a gold-digger in Australia's gold-fields. As a result of his experience in dealing with gold prospectors, young Larnach opened several branches for the Bank of New South Wales around Melbourne, these often being little more than a canvas tent and a strong-box guarded by a pair of gun-toting security men.

In 1859 Larnach married a 17-year-old French heiress, Elizabeth Jane Guise, in Melbourne. Soon after, when gold was discovered in Otago, he sailed for Dunedin to take advantage of the gold-rush and founded the First Bank of Otago for some London investors.

Larnach made money in other speculative ventures, including wheat, wool and refrigeration. As a status symbol he built for himself a beautiful castle, inspired by a panoramic view of Otago Harbour he happened upon while walking with his son, Donald. Classified as Gothic Revival in style, the building features elements found in many Scottish castles, such as crenellated balconies and turrets, but also evident is the influence of Australian Victoriana homesteads, in twin, two-tiered gingerbread verandas either side of the keep. A talented architect, R.A. Lawson, came from Scotland to oversee the project, and subsequently made a name for himself designing commercial buildings in Dunedin and Oamaru. It took 200 workmen three years to build the shell of the castle, and it was another 12 years before the interior was completely furnished, craftsmen being brought in from Scotland and France to install fine woodwork and fabrics.

Unfortunately, Larnach's domestic and business life took a chaotic turn, and, racked with embarrassment over a family scandal, he shot himself through the temple in Wellington's Parliamentary Buildings. It is said that his third young wife was having an affair with his youngest son by a previous marriage, and this was compounded by worry about bankruptcy following a crash in the wheat market. He left six children – two sons and four daughters.

Following their father's death the children sold the castle to the government. Until 1918 it was used as a hospital for mental patients and injured veterans of the First World War; meanwhile, abandoned, the gardens reverted to wilderness. After changing owners several more times it was bought by Margaret Barker and her husband in 1967. As Margaret explains: "My husband and I bought Larnach Castle as a

LEFT: *South-facing belvedere provides a spectacular view of Otago Harbour through the dark, spreading branches of macrocarpa which help shelter the garden from high winds.*

family home. But for me it was also an important conservation project, and my first priority was to repair the fabric of the building. Simultaneously I also worked at restoring the gardens, and now that the building restoration is completed, I am fully focused on expanding the garden."

Margaret's first improvements to the grounds included a clean-up of a shade garden at the rear of the castle, a sunny rock garden and some rhododendron slopes. She also added an enclosed perennial garden, a laburnum tunnel, sweeps of daffodils and a herb garden. Dotted about are whimsical figures from *Alice's Adventures in Wonderland*, including a bust of the Duchess in the herb garden and the Queen of Hearts' throne at the end of a fern-fringed avenue. Says Margaret of the future: "We are supporters of Dunedin's rhododendron festival, but we don't want to be known only for rhododendrons. I recently took a trip through Chile and realised that a lot of South American plants are related to New Zealand species, and will do very well here. So I am creating a special southern hemisphere garden with an emphasis on plants like Chilean puyas, a large spiny succulent with jade-green flowers from the Andes, so visitors can see a rich diversity."

Margaret has also installed a boardwalk and belvedere on a south-facing slope to provide spectacular views across Otago Harbour, having moved some tall rhododendrons that were in the way. She is a self-taught gardener, having inherited her interest from her mother, and is keenly interested in art. She employs three full-time gardeners and encourages visitors to stay overnight in lodgings overlooking the harbour.

"Money buys culture," she explains as bus-loads of tourists from all over the world file into the castle for guided tours before spilling into the gardens. "Without the gold-rush there would have been no Larnach Castle in the first place. When I bought the property it was in a shambles, and now it just thrills me to realise that contributions from visitors continue to help me save an important historical New Zealand landmark."

LEFT: *Lanarch Castle framed by the branches of a macrocarpa, its trunk encircled with daffodils in early spring.*

LEFT, TOP TO BOTTOM: *Decorative temple serves as a rain shelter; Rhododendron slope is gradually being transformed into a display garden for southern hemisphere plants, especially natives of Chile; Mixed shrub border of mostly New Zealand native plants encircles a sunny lawn, with mossy scabweed* (Scleranthus uniflorus) *prominent in the foreground.*

Pukemara Garden

A Native Plants Garden

Cor Fluit was born in Rotterdam, Holland, into a family who
had been Zeeland farmers for several generations. In 1950,
answering a call for skilled tradesmen to work on the
construction of the Roxburgh hydro-dam, he emigrated to New
Zealand, where he met his wife, Helen. After the dam had been
completed, he went to work for his father-in-law, who ran
nearby Moa Seed Farm.

Cor spent 19 years as a seed-grower, including the Second
World War, when he helped the farm produce tonnes of
vegetable seed for food production to aid the war effort,
especially parsnips and carrots destined for North Island farmers.
After the war, demand for vegetable seed declined, so the farm
switched to flower-seed production, with an emphasis on sweet
peas, which were popular among home gardeners in Australia
and Britain as well as in New Zealand. Eventually, however, in
1958, declining demand and competition from growing facilities
in California caused Moa Seed Farm to close, though the old
120-year-old stone seed house and homestead survive as a
restaurant at Dumbarton.

Cor and Helen moved to their present home, Pukemara – meaning "cultivated hill" – Cor working first as a groundsman at Glenfalloch Woodland Garden, near Anderson's Bay, on the Otago Peninsula, and then at nearby Larnach Castle. During their spare time, the couple indulged an interest in New Zealand native plants, including alpines, by developing a beautiful hillside garden behind their house, with additional space devoted to a bountiful vegetable garden on flat ground at the front.

"We had no money, but we lived rich," is how Helen sums up their lifestyle, for they made themselves largely self-sufficient, raising chickens, ducks and a pair of pigs, along with a menagerie of parrots, pheasants, a bad-tempered sulphur-crested cockatoo and a mild-mannered donkey.

"Over the years, we have had lots of offers to buy the donkey," Helen says, "but when people realise they can't have the donkey without the cockatoo, they change their minds."

Helen recalls Cor joking that the secret to maintaining a successful garden was to do all the planting while you were young and fit, so by the time you reached retirement, all you had to do was keep up with the pruning. A sign in the garden emphasises the point. It reads, "Such gardens are not made by singing 'Oh, how beautiful!' and sitting in the shade."

Sadly, Cor lost a battle with cancer in January 2002, but Helen has continued to cultivate the garden with the help of a daughter and her family, who live in Dunedin.

Another daughter, who graduated from Massey University as a horticulturist, is now working at the restored garden of Aberglasny, in Wales. Money for the restoration was provided by an American philanthropist, John Cabot, who recently purchased land in New Zealand for an ambitious native-plants garden and sought help from Cor in collecting certain specimens.

Many foreign visitors have sought the Fluits' expertise in growing alpines, which can be temperamental. The curator of an alpine house in Frankfurt, Germany, wondered why her plants were dying despite their climate-controlled environment. Cor suggested she install two large fans at opposite ends of the house and turn them on, first one and then the other, to simulate a change of wind direction each

day. The Fluits believed their own alpine garden, at the top of their property, thrived because the wind blew alternately off the ocean and off the land. The curator later wrote that Cor's suggestion worked.

Among the Fluits' favourite alpine treasures at Pukemara are silver-leaved daisy-flowered celmisias, which grow at altitudes of up to 1200 metres in the Southern Alps, and the crimson-flowering Poor Knights lily (*Xeronema callistemon*), which needs to be root-bound in a pot or cleft of rock to flower successfully. Also flourishing are the yellow-flowering spear grass (*Aciphylla squarrosa*) and a dwarf rata – no more than two-thirds of a metre high after 20 years of growth – that produces a perfect cushion of crimson blooms. Remarkably, the latter is not a tree rata but a vining rata (*Metrosideros fulgens*).

Other prides of the garden are frost-tender *Jovellana violacea*, a bushy Chilean perennial with masses of blue thimble-like flowers, and a plant that looks as if it's giving off a shower of sparks – *Hebe hulkeana*. Known commonly as New Zealand lilac, this produces clouds of glittering, pale-lavender flowers, but is still little appreciated by New Zealanders as a decorative garden plant.

As well as Cor's many talents as a gardener, Helen is proud of his role in the protection of local yellow-eyed penguins. She recalls how he persuaded the Department of Conservation to preserve the swimming birds' nesting sites. "When he realised the colonies needed fences to keep out stray dogs and cattle, the department first said they had no budget, but when Cor interested a rival department in taking action, DoC came around."

Among important visitors to the Fluits' garden has been BBC gardens commentator Peter Seabrook, who hosted a

segment on Pukemara for America's popular *Victory Garden* television show. Helen remembers Cor asking why a Brit was hosting an American television show. The show was syndicated to the BBC, he learnt, who demanded the appearance of a British garden expert every week. Helen also recalls how the crew laboured to make the garden look better for the camera when Cor and she thought it needed no embellishment.

Dr Ellen Henke, an American garden personality and travel guide who leads tours round New Zealand, admires Helen's determination to keep Pukemara looking good. "Cor's passing has left a big gap in Helen's life, but she hasn't had time to be lonely. Helen was a major driving force for Cor in the garden. She is determined to keep it the way Cor would have wanted. Even the vegie garden is about right now."

Previous page top left *Good natured donkey with sheltered vegetable garden in background.*
Previous page right: *Flowering speargrass (*Acyphilla squarrosa*) at the highest point in the garden, with Pacific coastline in the distance. Insets: flower cluster of red kaka beak (*Clianthus puniceus*) and rare dwarf form of rata vine (*Metrosideros fulgens*).*
Opposite left: *Entrance to the hillside garden with New Zealand lilac (*Hebe hulkeana*) backlit at the front door.*
Opposite right: *Sand tussock (*Poa littorosa*) makes a striking accent plant midway up the hillside garden.*
Above left: *Overall view of Pukemara from a nearby hilltop.*
Above right: *Grassy path leading through mixed shrub and perennial plantings to a chicken coop.*

Lindsay Crooks' Sculpture Garden

An Artist in the Garden

There is an age-old controversy about art in the garden, argued over by horticulturists and curators of art, which New Zealand artist Lindsay Crooks finds amusing. "Though gardening is considered an art when plants are used to produce colour, form and texture in a landscape, curators don't usually like flowering plants to detract from art collections, and so sculpture gardens tend to be mostly foliage gardens to provide green backdrops, or monotonous walled expanses with niches against which to admire sculpture. Also, it is the ephemeral quality of gardens that often causes us to overlook the art of gardens."

ABOVE: *"The Planter" working among calendulas.*
RIGHT, CLOCKWISE FROM TOP LEFT: *"The Fisherman" with catch among poker plants and geraniums with Pacific coastline in background; "The Sunbather" screened from the road by hydrangeas, geraniums and variegated New Zealand flax; "Mackenzie on the Run" commemorates a famous Scottish immigrant accused of stealing sheep, running among sweet alyssum; "New Zealand Madonna" on the surfing beach below the main house.*

Lindsay is one of New Zealand's most admired artists, and perhaps he more than anyone else in the country has created a successful partnership between studio art and garden. A former art teacher at the University of Otago, he adopts a wide range of styles in his paintings, from abstract art composed of vivid geometric brushstrokes to highly animated scenes celebrating energetic New Zealanders at work and play.

One of Lindsay's favourite local public places for finding motifs is the Dunedin Botanic Garden. As he explains: "I like to paint a precious moment of time, of people or objects interacting – not from photographs, but from observing a scene intimately. I was admiring some photographs of autumn foliage in a book on US gardens, and went to Dunedin searching for similar scenes of trees with russet-coloured leaves. I suddenly saw what I wanted to evoke a sense of autumn in the landscape. They were clipped evergreen hedges presenting bold geometric shapes under curtains of yellow, orange and red foliage from tall deciduous trees. That scene was the inspiration for an entire series of the Dunedin Botanic Garden in autumn."

However, Lindsay's most endearing work is a series of three-dimensional animated sculptures of people working or having fun, many of the most whimsical figures perfectly at home in his small, colourful flower-and-vegetable garden next to Brighton beach, south of Dunedin.

Only a narrow coast road and a strip of sand dunes separate Lindsay's property from rolling surf. Indeed, it was the prospect of jumping out of bed in the morning to surf Pacific rollers that originally attracted Lindsay and his wife, Janet, also an artist, to the property. Janet, whose art tends to celebrate the New Zealand landscape and New Zealand women, shares Lindsay's love of plants. Though exposure to wind and drifting sand makes gardening in the small fenced front yard a challenge, it is made possible by the addition of vast quantities of organic matter to the sandy soil, and a sheltering hedge of the salt-tolerant taupata (*Coprosma repens*).

The organic matter is mostly composted kitchen waste and garden debris, kelp from the tide-line and barrow-loads of horse manure from local stables. Janet believes the kelp, rich in minerals, contributes not only to the large size but also to the flavour and nutritional content of the cabbages, Brussels sprouts, rainbow chard and kumara that thrive within easy reach of the kitchen.

Clumps of nasturtiums and calendulas rub shoulders with the vegetables, and their edible flowers find their way into tossed salads composed of home-grown ingredients. Independent flower-beds of mixed perennials and annuals provide a succession of colour in summer. Red bee balm, red-hot pokers and gleaming white Shasta daisies flaunt sturdy, wind-resistant flower stems over cushions of African daisies, while a bush of fire-engine-red geraniums and purple

hydrangea heads mingle their globular flowers so they appear grafted onto a single plant. Cobalt-blue gates and fences not only heighten the colour spectacle, they also echo the blue of the ocean and the grey-blue walls of the extraordinary house and gallery, of similar design to the Art-Deco ticket office of the 1925–26 New Zealand and South Seas International Exhibition at Dunedin's Logan Park.

While Lindsay plants for bold colour harmonies, Janet seeks combinations of fragrant plants, hence the presence of lemon- and rose-scented geraniums, spicy rosemary and apple-scented feverfew. To step into their garden is like stepping into one of their paintings, on account not only of the three-dimensional figures placed strategically about the property, but also of the vibrant colours of garments strung along the washing line, the overall effect heightened by the intense reflectivity of the nearby beach.

Lindsay's sculptures and paintings show a zest for living, many of them dealing with romance and gardening. "The Planter" is a sculpture of a young man using a garden fork with athletic dexterity to uproot some turnips, and is placed, appropriately, between a row of silver beets and a row of cauliflowers. "The Sunbather" is a bronzed, nude, vivacious young woman meditating on a red beach blanket, while "The Weeder" is an angelic, slender, flaxen-haired young woman wielding a red bucket and modestly covered in a long grey skirt.

Like the paintings of Renoir, of beautiful plump women with rosy complexions and expressions of contentment, Lindsay's paintings are buoyant celebrations of simple pleasures. His garden, too – small and carefully composed, and a fine setting for his sculptures – evokes a sense of happiness and close communion with nature.

LEFT TO RIGHT: *"The Weeder" works beside a stepping stone path, among violas, sea pinks and white candytuft; "The Lovers" occupy a secluded niche beside a clump of variegated New Zealand flax, at the front of the main house; Big-leaf hydrangea and vigorous geranium intermingle their blooms in the front garden; A more youthful version of "The Planter" decorates the vegetable garden.*

Maple Glen

A Garden in the Land of the Giant Moa

If there were a competition for New Zealand's most beautiful garden, Maple Glen would most probably win. This four-hectare property is to New Zealand what the Beth Chatto Gardens are to Great Britain and Monet's garden in Giverny is to France – "a garden to knock your socks off", as the British would say; or "*la crème de la crème*", in French parlance. Add to its many fine qualities the fact that it is one of the most southerly of New Zealand's great gardens, at the edge of the coastal wilderness of the Catlins Forest Park, and its existence is all the more remarkable.

Like Bodnant Garden, in North Wales, Maple Glen encompasses an entire valley, including within its bounds shady woodland, sunny meadows, dry slopes, and a series of ponds and boggy hollows connected by spring-fed streams.

ABOVE: *An emu, relative of the extinct moa, has the run of the garden.*
RIGHT: *View from the main house over the valley garden where island beds criss-cross the slopes, the plantings mostly composed of evergreens, maples and a collection of Scottish heathers.*

The passion of mainly one person – Muriel Davison, lent invaluable help by her husband, Rob, and their son – it is full of wonderful plant partnerships and colour harmonies.

Muriel and Rob married in the mid-1960s and bought a farmhouse overlooking an overgrown gully between the agricultural settlement of Wyndham and the port of Bluff. Muriel's first impression of the place was coloured by the weather. "We are at the bottom of the world, and there isn't much between us and the South Pole except ocean, so the winds that blow in from the Antarctic can be brutal. Not the kind of place you'd choose to create a garden."

The couple doggedly milked cows for ten years to pay the mortgage, then turned to sheep-farming. To eke out the family budget, Muriel erected some manuka wattle fences as a wind cushion and began growing vegetables on terraced beds along the steep slope of the gully. She discovered that just a few metres down from the brow the wind dropped off noticeably. "I remember thinking how it seemed to offer sufficient shelter to be more adventurous," she says. "Some native flax to provide an additional buffer, and a rim of trees to further dissipate the wind, and I was ready to experiment with some wind-resistant ornamentals."

She knew that heathers could be grown in exposed areas if the soil was sufficiently acid, which it was. She selected English, Irish and Scottish varieties reputed for their toughness. These formed cushions of bright colour in summer, and they were good companions for selections of wind-resistant conifers, especially junipers and false cypress. The heathers and conifers thrived, encouraging Muriel to be more ambitious. "I was hampered only by my lack of gardening experience," she says "so I joined plant societies in England and Scotland, and began ordering seeds by mail. One of them, the Hardy Plant Society, had a seed exchange programme, and I remember I was able to purchase a hundred packets of choice varieties for tuppence apiece."

PREVIOUS PAGE: *Panoramic side view of the valley garden, with fragrant deciduous azaleas massed to provide bright colour.*
LEFT: *Bog garden massed with 'Inshriach' hybrid primulas, grown from seed imported from an Aviemore nursery in the Scottish Highlands. Hybrid rhododendrons planted along the stream bank in well-drained soil are the perfect accompaniment.*
ABOVE RIGHT: *Clematis 'Nelly Moser' grows through the branches of an 'Exbury' hybrid azalea.*
RIGHT: *View through larches, pruned high of side branches, to reveal one of several wildlife ponds, and a hillside of rhododendrons.*

She began taking cuttings of trees and shrubs from her parents' house across the nearby Mataura River, and concentrated on collecting maples, which she realised would produce spectacular autumn colours as well as fleecy foliage effects in spring and summer.

Rob borrowed a bulldozer and dug the series of ponds, and all manner of water fowl flocked in – ducks, geese, even swans, many of them nesting at the water's edge and among the heather. At first, Muriel had a plan to landscape around the ponds and up the sides of the gully in a radiating pattern like the spokes of a wheel, but she decided this would look too contrived, and found it more satisfying simply to follow the trails made by sheep, creating terraced beds as she went along.

"Making their zigzag trails into turf paths and following the contours of the land produced a much better result," Muriel recalls. "Each level of success encouraged me to new challenges. Daffodils of course are foolproof, and we now have tens of thousands." A seedling miniature daffodil that appeared as a volunteer she recognised as distinct and registered it under the name 'Little Goldfinch', making it available at a nursery she had established adjacent to the garden to help pay for its upkeep.

Eventually, Muriel decided to replace the old farmhouse with a new building, and hired architect Peter Baxter to build it, expressing great satisfaction at the results.

"It's the only structure on the property, and it dominates the garden from its situation on the highest point, but its modern design and all-white façade surprises a lot of people, who think we should have settled for something more rustic. Some people say it looks like the bridge of an ocean cruise ship and feel it's out of place, but I like its clean, modern, curving lines and the panoramic views from its cantilevered balconies. It's a surprise element and a good contrast for so large a garden. I think the architect gave us exactly what I wanted. Besides, straight lines are not natural in gardens."

The clean, curving lines and plain white walls are softened by hanging plants which cascade from deep planters hidden in the walls' double structure, the curtains of vegetation helping to blend the house with the garden.

Another of Muriel's passions is birds, and she fondly remembers how a pair of goldfinches always used to build their nest in a rose bush at her parents' home. Goldfinches galore nest at Maple Glen, which they share with more exotic birds that must be caged at night but are free to fly about the garden during daylight. All it takes is a whistle from Muriel for rosy-cheeked yellow lorikeets, green parakeets and blue love-birds to appear in a whirr of wings, settle affectionately on her shoulders and start nibbling her ear-lobes in hope of a hand-out. "We use no insecticides in the garden," she explains.

"They could be harmful to the birds, which keep the insects under control."

Swans and geese breed on the ponds, along with feisty, iridescent pukeko. In a meadow at the far end of the gully are emus, with large black eyes, long black eyelashes and a sensual expression that could melt butter. Foraging among clumps of rhododendron, and emitting a booming call when approached by visitors, they might be mistaken for giant moa.

One of Muriel's favourite plants is the giant Himalayan lily (*Cardiocrinum giganteum*). She grew her first specimens from seed, waiting seven years for them to grow large enough to bloom – up to three metres tall, with the top third of the flower stem occupied by long, white pendant trumpets with maroon centres. "Now they seed themselves wherever there is shade and deep leaf-mould," Muriel notes with pleasure.

The rare Himalayan blue poppy is another perennial resident, flaunting its sky-blue taffeta-like petals among cheerful yellow candelabra primulas. Muriel explains how to maintain it: "To keep the blue poppy perennial it is essential to pinch out the first flower spike. Otherwise it expends all its energy on seed production, and dies after its first flowering. But pinching out that first bloom encourages stronger root growth for a repeat flowering display in subsequent years."

Asked if the garden had ever been featured on the *Maggie's Garden Show*, Muriel replies, "Yes, but they came in winter when all we had in bloom was snowdrops!" Even so, the resulting footage made the garden look fabulous, because Maple Glen has such good bones and a maturity that gives it distinction in any season. The attention paid to growing trees with decorative bark, to maintaining a collection of choice evergreen conifers with blue and yellow foliage, to billowing broad-leaved evergreens such as rhododendrons, to deciduous trees that etch a tracery of branches against the sky, and to ribbon-like grass paths that follow the contours of the landscape, ensures Maple Glen is a garden for all seasons – even in the depths of winter, when most flowering plants lie dormant.

LEFT: *Japanese flowering cherry overhangs a grassy path carpeted with spent petals.*

Speight Gardens

Soar Like an Eagle

In 1986, after farming in rural hill country south of Te Anau, David and Mairi Speight decided to move to the Queenstown area when their children declined the opportunity to continue the business. They sold everything and took up residence on a four-hectare property they owned near Speargrass Flat, in the valley between the soaring Remarkables range and Coronet Peak. David was attracted to the valley through his interest in soaring, or gliding. "There is no better place in all of New Zealand for flying of all kinds," he insists.

ABOVE: *Gold mining implements decorate a birch grove massed with bluebells.*
RIGHT: *Overall view of Speight Gardens with deodar cedar among hedges of hornbeam that create self-contained garden rooms.*

"Although at first I envisaged a soaring port on the land, I anticipated problems from the local planning authorities, and when I discovered the airport at Omarama I found it a perfectly suitable alternative. Within moments of take-off I can unhitch from the tow-plane and glide like an eagle over magnificent snow-capped peaks, unpopulated green valleys and the aquamarine waters of Lake Wakatipu. There is no engine noise from a glider, just the quiet whoosh of wind, and it's the closest you can get to being a bird. The sense of peace and freedom is exhilarating."

David has participated in the annual Warbirds Over Wanaka International Air Show, at which pilots of historic planes gather to fly Tiger Moths, Spitfires and Messerschmidts, even staging mock dogfights for the spectators' entertainment. "It's a big tourist attraction now," he says.

Mairi embraced the site because she and David had recently toured British gardens. As she says: "It was at a time when gardening was the in thing in New Zealand, and I wanted to create a beautiful garden that was unique to New Zealand not so much from the plantings, but by having a formal garden in a dramatic setting of long views and high mountains."

To help her get started, Mairi enlisted the expertise of Dunedin florist Peter Johnstone, who immediately saw the potential for a spectacular garden and poured his heart into designing a formal layout that broke up the informality at the edges. "We went on from there, developing the garden in stages," recalls Mairi.

Thick hedges of hornbeam, yew and laurel were planted to define a series of interconnected garden "rooms", each with a different theme, including a rose garden containing a large collection of David Austin varieties, and a colour wheel of perennials divided into segments of blue, red, white, yellow, orange and pink. A large pergola supports a collection of clematis vines, their blooms mingling with those of wisteria and climbing roses. Low hedges of lavender edge many of the beds, which are laid out along a broad, curving main axis.

A house with a low profile and wide picture windows, designed by Queenstown architect John Blair, was built on a ridge overlooking the garden.

"Mairi is largely responsible for the plantings," explains David. "We generally have heavy frosts in winter, and even light dustings of snow, so the site is ideal for hardy English perennials and English roses. With flowering trees, we overplanted a lot, thinking that we had to compensate for

LEFT: *Doublefile viburnum (*Viburnum plicatum tomentosum*) mingles its blooms with those of a rhododendron in the shade of a weeping willow, helping to frame a sunny vista with a path of flagstone slabs coursing through.*

heavy losses, but we actually lost very little, and so now the maturity of all those trees makes a bigger impact than we expected. I helped Mairi by mowing the lawns and putting in irrigation, and we both worked on the massive flagstone walk at the termination of the main axis."

Flowering begins in early spring with drifts of daffodils and clouds of cherry blossom across a sunny meadow dotted with the black silhouettes of sheep. "We got the idea from a trip to France," David recalls. "We laughed out loud when we saw similar sheep 'grazing' on a busy French roundabout, and straightaway had a metalworking factory in Invercargill make some for us."

Other unusual structural embellishments include a set of large beige pottery jars marked "sulphuric acid" placed along a stairway leading to a belvedere. They came from a cheese factory, which used the contents for cleaning. There is also a collection of rusty steel gold-mining implements in a birch grove under-planted with bluebells. David explains: "We don't like ostentation in a garden, but some decorative accents and focal points are needed so there are contrasts of texture and form among the plants. The gold-mining artefacts add an understated sculptural quality, and are appropriate because of the importance of the gold-rush to opening up this part of the country."

Another important aspect of local history – liquid gold, you might say – accounts for the garden's name. This was conferred in honour of David's grandfather, who founded Speight's Brewery – "The Pride of the South" – although this has since become a public company.

Mairi and David have recently sold the property to people from Auckland keen to maintain the garden, but have not moved far. As David explains: "We have completed a new home on a ridge above the garden, and are still able to enjoy it from a more elevated position. Also, I continue to soar over the valley and the garden, and watch its continued progress from the air."

OPPOSITE TOP LEFT: *Flagstone path through a grove of Japanese cherries and rhododendrons to a sunny circular lawn bordered with bearded irises.*
LEFT: *Spires of white lupin and cushion of English thyme backlit by the sun. Randomly placed pottery jars provide decorative embellishment.*
ABOVE: *Colourful perennial border bright with bearded irises and lupins, with a golden-leaf locust creating a splashy lawn accent in the background.*

Lake Hawea Station

An Alfred Buxton Original

Lake Hawea Station encompasses 11,300 hectares of steep mountains and rugged shoreline on the south-east corner of Lake Hawea. It was established in 1908 by the Kingan family for two sons, William and John, but within a year the partnership was dissolved, allowing Jessie Kingan and her husband, Jack Rowley, to become the new owners. The couple lived in a two-room hut moved from a neighbouring sheep station, enlarging it as the years passed and the station prospered. Conditions were harsh. The surrounding mountains were largely bare of trees, and rabbits ate everything green in sight, while their burrows were a menace to livestock.

ABOVE: *Rustic bench in the sunken rose garden.*
RIGHT: *View from the house looking across the front lawn to Lake Hawea past a clump of* Euphorbia griffithii *and weeping Camperdown elm.*

Jack and Jessie had seven children – four sons and three daughters – and Jessie fought the sense of desolation the place gave her by gardening and entertaining an endless procession of visitors. In 1935, when the homestead was destroyed by fire, the couple decided to build anew and engage the services of Christchurch landscape architect the late Alfred Buxton to establish a more ambitious garden. Buxton was at the height of his popularity, and a garden designed by him was considered a status symbol, although what Jessie sought most was a solid, professional design within which to exercise her green fingers.

The homestead passed to the couple's third son, Jim, who married Fiona Pearse in 1942, Fiona taking on the responsibility of preserving Buxton's landscape. She and Jim in turn had three sons and three daughters. Tom, the middle son, remembers lots of stories of Buxton's visit to the property, and he treasures a book of Buxton's landscape projects entitled *Colonial Landscape Designer Alfred Buxton*, by Rupert Tipples, in which the Lake Hawea Station garden is featured. Tom married Adrienne McRae in 1972, and the two of them lived in a cottage next to the homestead, eventually moving in to the main residence with their three sons when their parents retired to a smaller residence in 1990, Jim subsequently passing away.

Adrienne is an avid gardener, but though the main features of Buxton's design have survived, she concedes it is a struggle to maintain his original plan. "The biggest problem was when a stream he used to create a series of small ponds dried up," she explains. "He had made the ponds a prominent feature of the front lawn, making two arched Japanese-style bridges out of poured concrete, the handrails featuring simulated branches. With a lack of water, I decided to make the ponds dry water features, lining the depressions with smooth riverstones, like dry water courses seen in Japanese gardens."

As before, the margins of the ponds feature ferns, hostas,

primulas and irises, framed by a weeping cherry, but Adrienne still harbours a desire to turn the ponds back into water features.

Adrienne admires Buxton's sunken rose garden, at the rear of the house, keeping it filled with heritage roses. Above, a rock garden brimming with perennials is another Buxton touch; likewise a short section of wall in front of the house, in which the gate and stone pillars define the entrance to a woodland garden Buxton filled mostly with ferns and rhododendrons.

Tom remembers his parents talking about Buxton's methods. "They were amazed at the number of truck-loads of plants he brought in. Lots of woody plants were always a big feature of his designs, and though he was awed by the surrounding landscape of steep mountain slopes and rock escarpments at the back of the house, the place begged for more trees. The starkness he partly relieved by a wide view of the lake, though Buxton sacrificed some of the view to make a long avenue of gum trees, which still survive. This screens the homestead from view until the last moment, when the driveway clears the top of the gum line."

Tom also remembers his father saying that when Buxton was there, he lived in the main house, and immersed himself so much in the project he would forget he was a house guest, refining his drawings and plant lists late into the night, then keeping the household awake by taking a bath at midnight and singing boisterously.

Adrienne is proud to be a third-generation Rowley living at Lake Hawea Station, and likes adding her own touches to the garden. These include a rustic, rose-covered wooden outhouse, the door of which opens to reveal an elegant ceramic commode, wallpapered surroundings and romantic light fixtures. She and Tom continue to enjoy the challenge of high-country farming, and encourage others to share the scenery and garden by making two cottages available for rent just beyond the boundaries of Buxton's endearing landscape.

OPPOSITE TOP LEFT: *View from top lawn over perennial border and sunken rose garden.*
LEFT: *Russell lupins create a bold accent atop a retaining wall against a spectacular background of mountains.*

195

The Mamakus

Gardening on a Gold-Prospector's Diggings

T he West Coast of the South Island is full of myths," says
Wendy Ross, whose woodland and water garden near the
re-created gold-mining settlement of Shantytown dispels the
most common misconception. "The biggest myth is that
cultivated plants are difficult to grow because of the high rainfall
of up to three metres a year. In fact, it's not the rain that's a
hindrance, but the sheer tenacity of the native bush to gain
dominance, and the aggressive nature of wekas, which forage in
the garden every day, uprooting young plants and prodding
crater-like holes in the lawns as they search for worms." A
protected species, the weka are trapped and released in a
local reserve.

ABOVE: *Brick patio with barbecue grill presents a surprise formal area.*
RIGHT: *Wildlife pond with a fountain spouting from a ponga tree fern stump, the
edges luxuriant with native flax, mamakus tree ferns, Japanese irises and bog
primulas.*

196

Wendy believes that splendid gardens on the West Coast are scarce because the majority of settlers there were hardened gold-prospectors, lumbermen and coal-miners. They began arriving in the 1860s, and were in a different social class from those who settled on the Canterbury Plains, on the other side of the Southern Alps, where farmers prospered and had time and money to establish elaborate pleasure gardens in a more benign climate.

As with others before them, it was gold that brought the Ross family from Christchurch to the Coast, through Arthur's Pass, in 1989. Robin, a manufacturing jeweller by trade, came to buy the precious commodity. He liked the six-and-a-half-hectare property for its proximity to his office, which he later expanded to serve as a retail jewellery shop. Buying gold involved seeking out diggers in remote areas of the bush and persuading them to sell their finds. Wendy remembers the times fondly. She often travelled with Robin, the two of them sometimes getting stuck on treacherous tracks, with no security escort for their valuable cargo of gold dust, flakes and nuggets, destined for export to an international bullion company in the USA.

The site the Rosses chose for their home was part flat paddock and part steep, bush-clad slope. It had been thoroughly worked over by gold prospectors: their diggings had turned an elevated plateau into a flax-choked bog, and they had littered the bush with narrow-gauge iron rails, digger buckets and bottle dumps. Gold can still be found on the nearby black-sand beach at Paroa, and even in the alluvial soil along two streams that run through the Rosses' garden, although only in small quantities.

Wendy's dream for the property, after the house had been built on a saddle of ground above the flat, was a bog-and-bush garden. She started along the curving driveway, planting along the edges, blending colonies of irises, arum lilies and giant gunneras with weeping rimu and feathery native tree ferns – notably mamaku, after which the property is named – so the driveway now forms a long, verdant tunnel.

The clayish, malnourished soil she supplemented with horse manure, sawdust from a local sawmill, and blood-and-bone meal from an abattoir. Once a bed is planted she doesn't dig it again, keeping weeds at bay by top-dressing each year with a fine bark-and-nutrient mixture trucked to the site.

Two ponds form the heart of the garden, connected by a stream and criss-crossed by bridges. A gazebo beside the larger pond provides a good rain shelter and a place to view luxuriant pond-side plantings, particularly Japanese water irises, astilbes, hostas and candelabra primulas.

Wendy feels the native bush adds a unique visual drama to her garden, referring to it as nature's bounty. She especially

likes the kamahi trees, with their mottled bark and snaking multiple trunks, and has cleared the under-bush to emphasise them. Although she spends six days a week tending her garden, with help from Robin mowing the grass, she still has time to pursue her interest in watercolour painting, which she considers a natural extension of her gardening activities. "Making a garden is painting a picture, and the picture is always changing," she explains with delight.

OPPOSITE: *A massive clump of Chilean rhubarb (*Gunnera manicata*) adds drama to explosions of foliage from native cabbage trees.*
TOP: *Japanese water irises and yellow bog primulas are good companions beside a gazebo overlooking the large pond.*
ABOVE: *Yellow bog primulas, a clump of watsonia, 'Royal Standard' hosta and a mass planting of lime-green lady's mantle fill an island bed to overflowing beside the larger wildlife pond.*

Stewart Island GARDENS

ALTHOUGH CAPTAIN COOK was the first European to sight Stewart Island, he did not land and thought that it was attached to the mainland. Separated from the South Island by 80 kilometres of often turbulent seas, Stewart Island is a mountainous land mass with over 1200 kilometres of indented coastline. The permanent population, concentrated around the settlement of Oban, in Halfmoon Bay, numbers less than 400, most of whom are engaged in fishing and tourism.

Stewart Island is a place noted for its sweet dawn chorus, tui and bellbirds providing a melodious counterpoint to the raucous cries of kaka. Sunrise and sunset can be a stunning palette of blazing colours, hence the island's Maori name – Rakiura, "land of glowing skies".

The Department of Conservation administers hundreds of kilometres of track and several huts. Much of the bush is classified as rain forest, and the island has a reputation for being wet and windy. Yet it is a marvellous place to garden in sheltered locations, for rainfall, though no greater than in Auckland, is fairly evenly distributed throughout the year, and winter frosts are only slight. The climate is deceptively mild – even nikau palms grow in sheltered areas.

LEFT: *View from The Nest, a Stewart Island coastal garden, showing parts of the native bush and an arc of sand with deep, clear green water known as Lonneker's Beach.*

The Garden Circle

New Zealand's Smallest Garden Club

Despite having only a small permanent population, Stewart Island boasts a number of beautiful private gardens, several of historical significance. Perhaps more remarkable, it has an active garden club – the Garden Circle. Founded in 1968, it has 15 members, their ages ranging from 40-ish to over 80, and all with beautiful gardens.

Accessible by air from Invercargill or ferry from Bluff, most of the gardens are coastal and within a mile walk of the wharf at Oban. Arrangements to visit the mostly private gardens can be made through several tour operators in Oban.

ABOVE: *Shirley poppies flower in a cottage garden.*
RIGHT: *A ravine at the back of Raylene Waddell's garden features an assortment of native tree ferns with white flowering New Zealand iris (*Libertia grandiflora*), blue flowering Chatham Island forget-me-nots, Himalayan rhododendrons and Chilean angel's trumpet (*Brugmansia sanguinea*), creating a supernatural Tolkien-like atmosphere.*

Ann Pullen's steeply sloping section of five-and-three-quarter hectares at Mill Inlet is typical of the kind of garden scattered about Stewart Island. Native bush extends almost to the house, and there is a sunny, spacious clearing rimmed with Chilean fire trees and Himalayan rhododendrons. Ann came to Stewart Island from Essex, in England, on a working holiday at the South Seas Hotel, met her future husband – a fisherman – and now works part time for the Department of Conservation (DoC) at its office in Oban. She frequently travels to rat-free Codfish Island to help in the project to save the kakapo from extinction. In the winter of 2001, she was involved in DoC's eradication of rats on Campbell Island. She recalls the sight of five helicopters flying in over the ocean to conduct the aerial spraying of poisoned bait as one of the most exhilarating she has ever seen. "Like witnessing the start of a military operation."

Most of Stewart Island's food supplies come from the mainland, via Bluff. Fresh vegetables often suffer during the journey, and aren't cheap, so, like many Stewart Islanders with gardens, Ann has a space for growing vegetables year-round, particularly salad greens and root crops.

Loraine Hansen's neat-as-a-pin coastal garden overlooks the wharf at Oban. The steep section is bordered by native bush, with rhododendrons planted along the edge. Paths connect several free-form lawns, and a boardwalk – arched over by *Clematis montana* – crosses a ravine to a clearing in the bush. Spectacular views from the picture windows in Loraine's living room include the red and white steeple of St Thomas's Presbyterian Church, atop Church Hill, and boats moored in Halfmoon Bay, where the catamaran ferry from Bluff plies back and forth several times a day.

Just round the corner, Loraine Squires cultivates a hillside garden called The Nest, at the top of which is a homestay cottage with a view of the sandy strand at Lonneker's Beach.

Murray and Nancy Scofield live at Ringaringa, on top of a hill with panoramic views of ocean, inlets and bush. Occupying about half a hectare of the property is a garden for the main house and a historic homestead, presently

LEFT: *View from the living room of The Norwegian House across the front lawn to native bush planted along the edge with rhododendrons.*

TOP RIGHT: *Portion of Peggy Wilson's garden merges seamlessly with her son and daughter-in-law's garden, with* Euphorbia griffithii *'Fireglow' resplendent in the foreground.*

RIGHT: *Pink flowering form of New Zealand manuka* (Leptospermum scoparium) *flowers in the native plants garden of Murray and Nancy Scofield, with Chatham Island speargrass in the foreground.*

unoccupied, built in 1888 by a family of early Stewart Island settlers, the Traills. "Our aim is to have a garden with plants that encourage bird-life," says Nancy. "And to care for rare plants introduced by Murray, who has a fondness for plants native to the Chatham Islands, including Chatham Island astelias and Chatham Island spear grass."

The Norwegian House is owned by Jeanette Mckay, a New Zealander who works in London for most of the year. Originally named Sjalyst, meaning "glimpse of the sea", it was prefabricated in Norway and shipped to the Rosshavet whaling company's repair base at Kaipipi Bay, in Paterson Inlet. Erected in 1927, it served as the manager's house until the whaling operation closed in the early 1930s.

In 1942, the house was purchased by Mab Prentice, dismantled and reassembled on Rankin Street, near Golden Bay. Mab developed a beautiful garden around free-form lawns, opened it to the public and lived in the house for 40 years. Bus tours would stop at her gate, and she had a small hut on the property where people could purchase her paintings and shellwork. The property today is a third of a hectare in area and surrounded by dense bush.

Raylene and Ronnie Waddell retired to Stewart Island after careers in teaching, and established a bed-and-breakfast at Glendaruel, just above the beach at Golden Bay. Their garden is new, most of it on the steep slope of a ravine. Access is via a zigzag path covered with iridescent paua shells, which are washed up on the local beaches whenever there's a storm. Behind a sheltering hedge at the top of the property Ronnie grows vegetables in raised beds.

Irene Denis – a past president of the Garden Circle – lives in a conspicuous A-frame house at the top of Oban's main street, with a commanding view of the harbour. As on most Stewart Island properties, a pair of gunneras stand sentinel at the driveway entrance. The garden slopes steeply and features some spectacular rhododendrons. Alongside the house is a secluded fernery, wooden trelliswork creating a cool, dark grotto filled with a wide range of native ferns. Irene's husband, Ron, is involved in the growing of paua pearls in tanks at a factory on the foreshore.

A founding member of the Garden Circle, Peggy Wilson has a house and garden overlooking Halfmoon Bay. The garden merges seamlessly with that of her son, Ian, and daughter-in-law, Phillipa, who run a water-taxi service and recently constructed a contemporary house overlooking the bay. Phillipa and Ian work continuously at landscaping their property, terracing a slope with views through macrocarpa down to the sea. They began work on the site in 1997, borrowing a tractor from Ian's grandfather to back-blade the bush. Ian is a sixth-generation Stewart Islander, and the family

owns the second-oldest stone house in New Zealand – a small one-room cottage called Ackers Stone House, at Harold Bay, where a reclusive Scotsman lived with his Maori wife and 12 children in the late 1820s.

Moturau Moana (meaning "leafy bushes by the sea") is located on a promontory overlooking Bragg Bay. In 1935, the late Noeline Baker built a house on the property, which she later donated with the grounds to the Department of Internal Affairs. In 1941 the house was acquired by the Forest Service and used as a ranger's residence.

Noeline was a controversial woman whose life spanned some of the most dramatic phases of women's liberation, including two world wars and the women's suffrage movement. Born into New Zealand's upper-middle class, she moved with her family to England, where she became concerned about the plight of women workers. She never married, but was devoted to her father – a surveyor – and often accompanied him on horseback into New Zealand's wilderness areas. She loved the landscape, and developed a passion for collecting native plants. After her father's death she chose to live in comparative isolation on Stewart Island, where she applied her energy to developing a beautiful botanical garden. However, she never completely severed her links with Britain, travelling regularly between the two island nations – "always missing the one she was away from," according to historian Leah Taylor. Sheila Natusch, who gardened for Noeline, remembers her formidable English accent, and accompanying her on plant-collecting trips throughout Stewart Island.

Though the house Noeline built burned down in 1967, the botanical garden is maintained as a public park. Broad grassy avenues lead through the beautiful collection of mature New Zealand plant species, a notable feature being a fern walk.

TOP LEFT: *Overall view of Ann's Place from the main house, showing a productive vegetable garden in the foreground and rhododendron slope merging into native bush in the background.*
TOP RIGHT: *Narrow winding paths lead through groves of rhododendrons and tree ferns in Loraine Hansen's garden.*
LEFT: *Corner of Ann's Place with Chatham Island forget-me-nots, yellow bog primulas and hybrid rhododendrons contrasting their vibrant blooms with encroaching native bush.*

Kau Tauranga

The Ultimate Coastal Garden

Olive Nilsen has what many Stewart Islanders would consider the most beautiful view on the island. Her home, Kau Tauranga (meaning "safe harbour"), sits snugly on a cliff above Oban's secluded Bathing Beach, with a steep bush walk leading to a powder-soft strand of yellow sand. Also within view of her living room are the horseshoe-shaped sandy beaches of Butterfield Beach and Bragg Bay, set in rocky bush-covered coves within the sheltered bight of Halfmoon Bay.

For many years Olive and her husband, Bruce, made a living crayfishing, sheep-farming and taking tourists on pleasure cruises. Now retired, Olive had difficulty adjusting to Bruce's death at the age of 79. To stave off boredom and prevent the property from becoming "a prison in paradise", she began pouring her energy into creating a unique coastal garden.

ABOVE: *Sheltered native plants garden features Stewart Island natives that sprang up naturally in other parts of the garden.*
RIGHT: *Mixed shrub border with deciduous azaleas prominent in the foreground and Halfmoon Bay's Bathing Beach in the background.*

Small and narrow – just a tenth of a hectare in area – it wraps around three sides of her cosy cottage. It features an English cottage garden at the front, a rock garden of mostly native plants on the east side, and a water garden facing north. Olive has an unheated greenhouse for propagating seeds and cuttings, and spends part of almost every day planting and transplanting.

The front yard is screened from the road by a dense hedge of willow, oak and beech trees. On the windward side, the property is sheltered by tall mutton-bird scrub (*Brachyglottis rotundifolia*), displaying large, leathery leaves and daisy-like flowers. The rectangle of informal garden between this and the house features mostly cottage-garden perennials such as poppies, lupins and delphiniums.

Olive's favourite flowering plant is fuchsia, because of its long bloom period, and she is fond of her azaleas and rhododendrons, although these flower for only a short time. There are five small pools on the property, all dug by Olive.

One is lined with concrete, the others with flexible plastic. They are planted with bog primulas and water lilies.

At the highest point of the east-facing part of the garden is a massive algae-and-moss-covered boulder. The lowest part features a derelict 1982 Ford Escort wagon. Positioned as though it has swerved off the driveway and crashed into the rocky ridge, it makes an appealing garden ornament. Originally red, its body is now painted brown with green icons representing indigenous Stewart Island plant species. Surrounding the car is a mixture of garden perennials and native plants, the curving edge of a perennial bed leading the eye to an arbour covered in variegated English ivy. The arbour provides access to the secluded garden of natives, which in turn provides access to a colourful cliff-top garden featuring a pond, a velvet-green lawn and rhododendrons.

Olive has never needed to purchase native plants or bring them in from the wild because they have appeared naturally in various parts of the property, from seeds blown in from the

bush. They include dracophyllum shrubs, lancewoods, mountain cabbage trees, rata and coprosma. When she spots a new treasure, Olive digs it up and moves it to a preferred position.

Olive finds Stewart Island a relatively easy place to garden provided there is shelter, which she has thanks to the front hedge and the native bush that bounds the rest of the property. She elaborates, "Because of the damp we have plenty of slugs, and rats can be a problem for vegetable plots, but most Stewart Island gardeners complain about the kaka, which like to sit in the trees and strip branches of bark and buds. We are a paradise for birds, with one of the largest remaining concentrations of kiwi, which live in the bush and forage for grubs."

"There's never a time of the year when you cannot have flowers in the garden. We have mild winters, and I can grow cauliflower all winter, also marguerite daisies and scented stocks. Daffodils bloom extravagantly, and at The Neck, where

my husband and I tended sheep for 20 years, they cover the hillsides by the thousand."

Olive and Bruce's time as crayfishers, when they would sail as far as Dusky and Chalky Sounds, in Fiordland, came before they took up sheep-farming. With her pleasure boat, Olive also took tourists on picnics around Paterson Inlet, including to her favourite spot – Post Office Cove, on Ulva Island, with its once beautiful garden.

BELOW LEFT: *Rock garden with arbour covered in a variegated English ivy, partnered by several dracophyllum shrubs with slender grass-like leaves and a tall mountain cabbage tree* (Cordyline indivisa)*, resembling a palm tree.*
BELOW RIGHT: *Derelict 1982 Ford Escort van, painted with plant icons, is used as a garden ornament, in a corner of the rock garden.*

"There were times I would take 60 visitors at a time to Post Office Cove, and the owners would let us brew a big kettle on the beach for cups of tea and a cauldron to cook paua picked from the rocks. Another favourite destination was Mason's Bay, on the desolate west side of the island. To get there I would take visitors through the Chocolate Swamp, where we would sometimes wade waist deep through the tannin-stained water. But it was worth it, because the swamp has a clean, invigorating aroma, and Mason's Bay is rimmed with miles of sand dunes. It was so pristine and secluded you didn't need a bathing suit to swim. Now, tourists can charter a plane and pilot to land on the beach in the morning, and they're picked up by boat from a jetty along Freshwater Creek in the late afternoon.

Stewart Island isn't what it used to be. Back when I was a schoolgirl the islanders were a more closely knit community, and even the tourists we would know by name because they were regular visitors – mostly farmers and fishermen from other parts of New Zealand. I remember Captain Turner, owner of Raroa house and garden, would organise film shows in the village hall of his wildlife series, and Noelene Baker, owner of Moturau Moana house and garden, would give picnics at Christmas in the grounds for children. Now they are both gone and their properties a shadow of what they used to be."

Olive has raised three daughters, two of whom live on Stewart Island, and she has a stepson who farms The Neck, the only remaining sheep station on the island. "Seven generations of my family have lived on Stewart Island," she says proudly. "My family came here from the Orkney Islands, and I can trace my ancestry to Robert the Bruce."

LEFT: *Water lily pool with a concentration of New Zealand native plants, including oioi, or jointed rush, several varieties of New Zealand flax and tussock grasses, and splashes of magenta from sea pinks. Beyond are the bush-clad cliffs of Halfmoon Bay.*

Raroa

Captain Turner's High Place

Many Stewart Islanders fondly remember Captain George Middleton Turner (1893–1973) as the perfect English gentleman. Born in Birmingham to a wealthy family, he studied at Oxford University before being commissioned captain in the British Territorial Army. While he was serving in France during the First World War, the crown of his head was blown off, but after extensive surgery he was able to lead a productive life with a metal plate to replace the shattered part of his cranium.

After an honourable discharge from the army, Captain Turner travelled the world seeking a place to settle down. Following a stint of sheep-farming in Australia, he discovered Stewart Island and fell in love with its wild beauty. He built a house atop a steep hillside overlooking Halfmoon Bay and proceeded to make a secluded garden of six inter-connecting "rooms".

ABOVE: *Spectacular tree-size rhododendron overlooks the community of Oban.*
RIGHT: *Entrance to Raroa, once considered the most beautiful garden in the South Pacific. Though this entrance to the property is private, nearby is the entrance to Fuchsia Walk, a public trail leading through the native bush to Golden Bay.*

He called his comfortable home Raroa, meaning "high place", and while he remained wealthy through inherited money, he earned a reputation as a skilful wildlife photographer and cinematographer. He not only documented every aspect of wildlife around New Zealand, but also created a valuable archival record of Stewart Island colonial life, including the practice of mutton-birding. His negatives and original film footage are now in the safekeeping of the Department of Conservation's (DoC) Southland Conservancy, while many of his black-and-white photographs are on display in the Stewart Island Museum, on Ayr Street.

Captain Turner eagerly explored and documented every part of Stewart Island, and also made frequent expeditions south to the Snares and the Auckland Islands. He explored the Three Kings Islands, off Cape Reinga, in 1934, and Codfish Island, off Stewart Island, in 1949, filming their indigenous flora and fauna. He married late in life, and with his vivacious young wife entertained government and diplomatic dignitaries from around the world. A walk through his garden was considered a special privilege. Captain Turner was delighted to show visitors not only the cultivated part of his eyrie, but also a beautiful bush trail he had created at the rear of the property, leading down to the beach at Golden Bay through kiwi-inhabited rain forest. In its prime, the captain's garden earned a reputation in military and diplomatic circles as the most beautiful in the South Pacific.

For the cultivated parts of the garden immediately surrounding his home, Captain Turner imported boat-loads of plants from the mainland, seeking out choice varieties of

European trees and shrubs to partner his favourite New Zealand natives, which included lancewoods, cabbage trees, mamaku tree ferns, rata and the world's southernmost kauri. The last of these he planted as a seedling in the 1920s, and today it stands 10 metres tall. Sheila Natusch worked as a gardener for the captain, and remembers his pride and pleasure at getting a pohutukawa – unlike rata, not a Stewart Island native – to thrive and flower. When kaka began ripping it apart, he couldn't decide which to protect, the tree or the birds.

Today, Raroa is a DoC staff residence. Although the present occupants value their privacy and discourage visitors, the house and garden can be seen from the wharf at Oban, especially in spring, when several large rhododendrons light up the hillside. Captain Turner's bush trail is maintained as a public footpath, called Fuchsia Walk, its verges overhung with fuchsia trees, tree ferns and wild orchids.

FAR LEFT: *View looking up the steeply sloping front lawn to the hillside garden where tree-size rhododendrons compete successfully with the native bush for light and elbow room. The creeper scrambling up a cabbage tree trunk is akakura (Metrosideros carminea), a vining rata.*
LEFT: *View from the top of the garden over the roof of the homestead to the wharf at Oban where ferries from the mainland arrive.*
BELOW: *Another high elevation view from the upper garden. The sinuous branches of a large rata tree mingle with the spiky foliage of native cabbage trees and the broad lustrous leaves of a rhododendron helping to create a beautiful foliage tapestry.*

Ulva Island Post Office

New Zealand's Most Southerly Private Garden

Ulva Island is a sanctuary of near-pristine wilderness in the mouth of Paterson Inlet. Except for a seven-and-a-quarter-hectare section of private land, it is maintained by the Department of Conservation, which has rid the island of rats so native plants and birds can flourish undisturbed. Visitors can enjoy several miles of nature trails that meander through lush rain forest.

Down a private track marked by an ornate metal gate at Post Office Cove is a small one-time post office building and a cluster of holiday cottages. The oldest buildings date back to 1872, when the first European residents, Charles and Jessie Traill, settled on the island. Although they and their daughter were the only inhabitants, living mostly off the bounty of the sea, their homestead was considered an ideal site for a post office because it was central to Stewart Island's scattered communities.

ABOVE: *The old post office building sheltered by native bush.*
RIGHT: *Post Office Cove seen through the branches of muttonbird scrub, the leaves of which were once used by sailors as postcards.*

The Traills' post office served the sawmillers, boat-builders and fishermen who lived in settlements around Paterson Inlet, many of them accessible only by sea, and whenever the mail-boat arrived from Bluff, which it did irregularly, the Traills flew a flag to notify people the mail was in. Many chose to call on Sunday, dressing in their best clothes for the occasion, so picking up the mail became a popular social occasion.

Early patrons of the post office also used the leathery leaves of mutton-bird scrub as postcards. Muttonbirds – or sooty shearwaters – raised their young in burrows among the plant's roots. The fluffy brown chicks were so well fed by their parents they grew larger than the adults, and were a delicacy to Maori and settlers alike. Smoked and roasted, they were the size of a duck, smelled of mutton during cooking, and tasted like kippered herring. The oval leaves of mutton-bird scrub are glossy on the upper surface and silvery, with a felt-like texture, underneath, allowing them to be written on with pencil or ink. They were used as a paper substitute mostly by visiting seamen, including whalers. With appropriate postage paid, they were accepted for mailing by the post office until it closed in 1923.

The Traills also cultivated a beautiful garden around the post office, planting macrocarpas for shelter, along with evergreen grandiflora magnolias and rhododendrons. Today, bush has reclaimed much of the garden, but remnants survive under the care of members of the Hunter, Bonner and Mackenzie families, who live on the mainland and use the cottages at weekends and for holidays.

The macrocarpas and rhododendrons have grown large, and colonies of flag iris and South American fuchsia flourish in company with one of New Zealand's rarest plant species, punui (*Stilbocarpa layallii*), which survives in its natural state only on Ulva Island, having been brought to the brink of extinction elsewhere through browsing by deer, possums and rats. Displaying clusters of glossy, parasol-shaped leaves, punui is closely related to the subantarctic-island megaherb known as Macquarie Island cabbage.

Today's owners of the Ulva Island post office inherited it from their grandmother, who bought it from the Traills. They delight in having family reunions at the holiday cottages, recalling their grandmother describing how crayfish were once so plentiful in the cove they used to crawl over each other in the kelp beds.

Inexpensive water taxis take visitors from Golden Bay across the narrow channel to Post Office Cove, where part of the historic building and garden can be seen from the wharf. However, visitors are asked to respect the privacy of the current owners by not passing through the gate.

OPPOSITE: *Privately owned Ulva Island Post Office seen from the public wharf at Ulva Island.*
BELOW LEFT: *One of New Zealand's rarest native plants, punui (Stilbocarpa lyallii), with lustrous heart-shaped ruffled leaves, growing beside a bush walk at the Ulva Island Post Office, in company with a mountain cabbage tree.*
BELOW RIGHT: *Outhouse in danger of being swallowed up by native bush at the historic Ulva Island Post Office.*

APPENDIX

Although the gardens featured in this book are privately owned, most are open to the public on a regular or limited basis. Some also offer homestays. For example, Rathmoy has a rental cottage with access to the garden, while Cliff-top has a rental apartment that not only has garden access but also enjoys spectacular views of the Kaikoura coastline and mountains.

NORTH ISLAND GARDENS

Butler Point, Mangonui, Northland. Garden and whaling museum open by appointment. Homestay also available. Call (09) 406 0660.

Horrell Garden, Kerikeri, Northland. Open during Kerikeri Gardens Week, in October. Call (09) 407 8546.

Bellevue Garden, Lang's Beach, Northland. Open by appointment. Call (09) 432 0465.

Westridge Garden, Titirangi, Auckland. Visits by appointment and during special charity weekends. Call (09) 530 8706.

Ayrlies, Whitford, Auckland. Open by appointment. Call (09) 530 8706.

Noel Scotting's Garden, Whitford, Auckland. Open by appointment. Call (09) 537 3499.

Trelinnoe Park, Napier. Open mid-August to mid-May. Call (06) 834 9703.

Ngamatea, Taihape–Napier Road. Rental house available. Call (06) 844 3396.

Titoki Point, Taihape. Open by appointment. Call (06) 388 0085.

Rathmoy Garden, Hunterville. Open by appointment. Rental cottage available. Call (06) 322 8334.

Glen Colyn, Kimbolton. Nursery open for retail plant sales. Call (06) 328 5901.

Cross Hills Gardens, Kimbolton. Open October through November, other times by appointment. Nursery open May to November. Call (06) 328 5797.

Pukemarama, Palmerston North. Open by appointment. Call (06) 324 8446.

Ngamamaku, New Plymouth. Open by appointment. Call (06) 752 7873.

Burnard Gardens, Waikanae. Open by appointment. Rental apartment available. Call (04) 526 7531.

Moss Green Garden, Lower Hutt. Open by appointment. Call (04) 526 7531.

SOUTH ISLAND GARDENS

Winterhome, Kekerengu. Open by appointment. Call (03) 319 6649.

Cliff-top, Kaikoura. Open by appointment. Call (03) 319 6649.

Robyn Kilty's Garden, Christchurch. Open by appointment. Call (03) 377 2802.

Gethsemane Gardens, Christchurch. Open year round. Call (03) 326 5848.

Ohinetahi, Governor's Bay. Open 10.00 a.m. to 4.00 p.m. weekdays, mid-September to 23 December and 7 January to end of March.

Tree Crop Farm, Akaroa. Open year round. Rental cottages available. Call (03) 304 7158.

Grehan Lea, Akaroa. Open by appointment. Call (03) 304 8600.

Trott's Garden, Ashburton. Open by appointment. Plant sales available. Call (03) 308 9530.

Parkside, Oamaru. Open by appointment. Call (03) 433 1134.

Larnach Castle, Dunedin. Castle and gardens open year round. Rental accommodation and plant sales available. Call (03) 476 1162.

Lindsay Crooks' Sculpture Garden, Brighton Beach. Garden and art gallery open at weekends. Call (03) 481 1805.

Maple Glen, Wyndham. Open by appointment. Plant sales available. Call (03) 206 4983.

Pukemara, Dunedin. Open by appointment. Call (03) 476 1162.

Speight Gardens, Queenstown. Open by appointment. Call (03) 442 8451.

Lake Hawea Station, Lake Hawea. Open by appointment. Rental cottage available. Call (03) 443 1744.

The Mamakus, Greymouth. Open by appointment. E-mail robinross@xtra.co.nz.

STEWART ISLAND

The Garden Circle, Halfmoon Bay. Gardens of members open by appointment. Homestays available. For Glendaruel Bed & Breakfast call (03) 219 1092 or e-mail r.r.waddell@xtra.co.nz.

Kau Tauranga, Oban. Open by appointment. Call (03) 219 1343.

Raroa, Oban. Garden not open to the public. Fuchsia Walk open dawn to dusk. Obtain trail map at DoC office on Main Street.

Ulva Island Post Office. Garden not open to the public, but can be viewed from wharf at Post Office Cove, where island bush walks begin.

Published 2003 by David Bateman Ltd,
30 Tarndale Grove, Albany, Auckland, New Zealand

ISBN 1-86953-555-3

Design Lesley Coomer/Creative Type Ltd
Printed in China through Colorcraft Ltd